USEFUL HANDBOOKS ON
ATHLETIC SPORTS.

Association Football

By J. L. JONES, *Welsh International Twenty Times, and Captain Tottenham Hotspurs, 1901-4.*

Cloth,
Price 1s.,
post free 1s. 2d.

A Complete Handbook to all Departments of the Game, with Rules and Explanation of the Offside Rule.

Rugby Football

By JEROME J. RAHILLY *(London Irish Rugby Football Club).* A Practical Handbook of the Game and How to Play It, together with Rules, etc. *Cloth,* **Price 1s.,** *post free* **1s. 2d.**

Training

For Athletics and General Health.

By HARRY ANDREWS, *Trainer of Montague A. Holbein, A. Shrubb, Frank Shorland, J. Butler, A. A. Chase, A. E. Walters, Platt-Betts, etc., etc.* *Cloth,* **Price 1s.,** *post free* **1s. 2d.** Some of the 20 Chapters are :—

CHAPTER I. TRAINING AND EXERCISE.—Ages for Training—The Best Years—Good at all Ages —For the Delicate —Walking Exercise — Unconscious Benefit — When to Walk— A Medical Opinion—The Rate of Walking.

CHAPTER III. SLEEP, BATHING, AND MEDICINE.

CHAPTER IV. — FOOD, DRINK, AND SMOKING.

Walking
A Practical Guide to Pedestrianism.

By C. LANG NEIL.

With Contributions by
W. J. STURGESS and W. GRIFFIN.
With Illustrations.

Cloth, **Price 1s.,** *post free* **1s. 2d.**

CONTENTS.—The Science of Walking—Walking of a Natural Kind — Athletic Walking — Walking with Bent Legs — Exertion in Walking—Training—Exercise in Training—Ages for Training—Massage, etc.—Care of the Feet — An Athlete's Clothing and Embrocation — Walking Tours — Mountaineering — Walking Records, etc., etc.

Dumb=bells, Clubs & Bar=bells
For Schools & Gymnasiums or Individuals.

BY
A. G. LAMMAS, *Army Gymnastic Staff.*

With 150 Illustrations.

Cloth, **Price 1s.,** *post free* **1s. 2d.**

Modern Physical Culture

By C. LANG NEIL.

With numerous Diagrams.

Cloth, **Price 1s.,** *post free* **1s. 2d.**

The Ling or Swedish System — The Macfadden System — The Vibration System — Sandow's System — Apollo's System—The Italian Hercules—Exercises with the Sandow Developer—Dumb-bells —Exercises on a Horizontal Bar fixed in a Doorway — Chest Development — Curative Exercises — Drink and Liquid Foods, etc.

The above volumes may be had of all Booksellers, or post free from the Publishers, C. Arthur Pearson, Ltd., 17-18 Henrietta Street, London, W.C.

TRAINING FOR ATHLETICS

AND GENERAL HEALTH

TRAINING

FOR ATHLETICS

AND GENERAL HEALTH

By

Harry Andrews

Trainer to

South London Harriers

and of

Montagu A. Holbein	A. Shrubb
Frank Shorland	J. Butler
A. A. Chase	A. E. Walters

Platt-Betts, etc. etc.

Fourth Impression

BLOOMSBURY

First published 1911 under the title *Training for Athletics and General Health* by C. Arthur Pearson Limited

Copyright © 2005 Octopus Publishing Group

This edition published by Bloomsbury Publishing in 2005

The moral right of the author has been asserted

Bloomsbury Publishing Plc, 36 Soho Square, London W1D 3QY

A CIP catalogue record for this book is available from the British Library

ISBN 0 7475 7907 5
ISBN-13 9780747579076

10 9 8 7 6 5 4 3 2 1

Printed by Clays Ltd, St Ives plc

All papers used by Bloomsbury Publishing are natural, recyclable products made from wood grown in well-managed forests. The manufacturing processes conform to the environmental regulations of the country of origin.

http://www.bloomsbury.com

It is advisable to check with your doctor before embarking on any exercise programme. A physician should be consulted in all matters relating to health. Neither the author nor the publisher can accept legal responsibility for any injury sustained while following the exercises.

Preface

I WRITE a book on training for several reasons. In the first place, I believe that there is room for a work by a practical trainer. I know of many volumes which touch at more or less length upon the subject, but these are almost all written by athletes, who have, of course, undergone periods of training, and whilst there is much that is good in their books, there are many little practical points which are overlooked.

The trainer has always attended to these for them, in fact it is part of training that they should be saved all thought about such details; hence, when they come to write upon the subject these points are omitted, simply because they have not been noticed.

Secondly, no books and very few trainers give sufficient prominence to what I consider perhaps the most important modern method of getting the body fit, namely, Massage. I lay the credit of two-thirds of the daily more numerous American successes to a right appreciation of massage.

Thirdly, so many clubmen and cyclists have asked me to put the result of my experience into a perma-

Preface

nent record, that I think there must be a desire for such a book.

Those who know me are well aware that I am not, and do not pose as, an educated man, and that the information which follows is the result of practical experience only. If I run counter to theories put forward by more learned people, my excuse is that I judge from results I have seen and tested, without having gone deeply into the why and the wherefore.

The book has been written at my dictation, and put on paper by one more accustomed to such work than I; at the same time I have taken care to see that my exact meaning has been preserved.

HARRY ANDREWS.

Crystal Palace Track,
London, S.E., 1903.

Contents

CHAPTER I

TRAINING AND EXERCISE

Ages for training—The best years—Good at all ages—For the delicate—Walking exercise—Unconscious benefit—When to walk—A medical opinion—The rate of walking .

CHAPTER II

MASSAGE

Massage, not glove-rubbing—American successes—Its objects—Removes bad flesh—Great boxer's opinion—For rheumatics —How to do it—To develop special muscles—After exercise —The face .

CHAPTER III

SLEEP, BATHING, AND MEDICINE

Nine hours for sleep—Importance of regularity—People who cannot sleep—The morning tub—Warm bath best—An unhealthy practice—Hot sea baths—Medicine—When to take it—Keep bowels open .

Contents

Contents

Contents

A Foreword

I BELIEVE that there are very few people who would not derive benefit from a moderate course of training; but as this book is, in many parts, devoted to the description of courses of preparation for special events, it is perhaps as well to commence with a word of warning.

Not every man is physically fit to go through the somewhat severe training necessary to achieve great things as an athlete.

Some may show signs of being gifted runners, who would yet be seriously injured if put through a regular stiff training, say for the half-mile race.

Weaknesses not necessarily an absolute Bar to Athletics.

Without wishing to damp anybody's athletic aspirations, I would strongly advise every man who is contemplating going into training first to consult his doctor as to his physical fitness generally, and with special reference to the particular class of feat he proposes to prepare for; and also as to the state of his heart, lungs, &c.

A Foreword

If the medical man certifies all well, the athlete can throw himself with much more confidence into his work than without such an assurance.

Then again, the doctor's examination may show a tendency to some local trouble, such as slight weakness of the lungs or heart, which, whilst not serious enough to stop training, it is important to be aware of, seeing that the subject can specially train to remedy the defect.

TRAINING FOR ATHLETICS

CHAPTER I

Training and Exercise

Ages for training—The best years—Good at all ages—For the delicate—Walking Exercise—Unconscious benefit—When to walk — A medical opinion — The rate of walking.

NOTHING under nineteen is my limit of age—I should perhaps say youth—for putting young men through training.

Under that age the more exercise and sports a boy goes in for the better, but he does not need training. His young body should always be as fit as it would be wise to train it to be.

Younger boys have been placed under me, and I have seen boys trained by others, but cannot record a case where one made any great after-success.

The Best Years.

The very best years for training are from twenty-three to twenty-seven. This latter age generally sees the end of a sprinter's career as a champion.

Long-distance men are more fortunate, for they can retain champion form right up to forty, and in a few cases to forty-five.

For the Delicate

In giving these ages, I am speaking of regular severe training for competitions amongst good men.

Training Good at all Ages.

Training for what I may term daily health—taking some particular sport and training for it, is, I am sure, good up to almost any age.

The man who has been an athlete, and more or less kept it up, can be going into training each spring when he is getting on into the sixties with benefit to himself.

For the Delicate.

In a moderate form, training is perhaps more important to the weakly than to any one else, but in their case medical advice should always be taken as to the form and extent of the training advisable.

Walking, which will be found throughout this book to be a prominent part of my system for every type of athletics, is invaluable to the delicate. Weak, contracted chests under its influence become expanded and healthy. It forces good long natural breathing, and the body sucks in benefit from the air so brought into it which could not otherwise have come its way.

Walking Exercise.

There is one form of exercise above all others for everyday health and for training, whatever the branch of sport entered upon may be.

It is in keeping with the rest of the beneficent provisions of Providence, that the very best exercise is walking, which we must all of us perforce indulge

When to Walk

in to a greater or less extent from the time after our entry into this world when first our legs are strong enough to carry us.

Be it for sprinting or cross-country running, rowing or boxing, jumping or heavy-weight lifting, it is all the same, walking is the exercise beneficial beyond all others.

Unconscious Benefit.

Softly, easily, unconsciously, but surely, walking gets at every muscle in the body.

No undue strain is cast upon the functions of any particular part, but all are affected for good.

The main reason why a man can rarely create records without having, at least when in training, to drop his regular employment, is that if he does not do so he must sacrifice the walking part of his preparation.

For athletes in training, I give hints as to the amounts of walking to be done according to their object, under the different chapters devoted to sprinting, long-distance work, boxing, &c., so I confine myself here to remarks on this exercise as a health-giver in daily life.

When to Walk.

A walk before breakfast, a mile out and a mile home every morning, is in my opinion worth all the medicine in the world.

To the average individual it will be quite a hard and gruelling task for the first fortnight; but if it is any consolation, let him take heart from this very fatigue, for it is the surest proof that he is in need of what he is doing.

The Rate of Walking

If a man's occupation allows of it, four or five miles may be negotiated between breakfast and dinner, and this is none too much.

After tea three or four miles.

This latter is the clerk's and business man's chance. The walk between breakfast and dinner is of necessity barred them, but there is nothing to prevent before breakfast and after tea pedestrianism.

A Medical Opinion.

I was one day discussing with a clever young doctor the pros and cons of several physical culture systems, when he broke in upon the argument, exclaiming vehemently: "Why should a man go in for any physical culture at all? Let him take a long walk in the country, or in one of the parks every evening for six months, and then retake his measurements, chest and limbs, and see if he has not improved all round as much as any system of culture will do for him in a like time."

The Rate of Walking.

As to speed. Don't worry to do any particular pace.

Speed in walking will come naturally to him who persists in long walks.

A man who in his first few outings does, say, three and a half miles an hour, will at the end of a couple or three weeks be going an average four without even noticing that he is any speedier than before.

Every one must find the speed which comes easiest to him. About four miles an hour is a good average.

CHAPTER II

Massage

*Massage, not glove-rubbing—American successes—Its objects
—Removes bad flesh—Great boxer's opinion—For rheu-
matics—How to do it—To develop special muscles—
After exercise—The face.*

IT is only in quite recent times that massage has come
to be estimated at anything like its true value in training, and even now its benefits are scarcely known
outside the ranks of a few first-rate trainers.

Personally I have no words of praise strong enough
to convey my appreciation of what it does for a man.
Every man I train has it after every exercise, which
means in most cases twice a day, and I feel confident
in stating that I do not believe a single one, who has
marked by experience its effect upon his muscles and
general system in one course of training, would ever
do without it in a future course of preparation for any
event.

Massage—Not Glove-Rubbing.

In speaking of massage, let not the reader confuse
it with the glove-rubbing, which has been for many
years universal amongst men in training. My father
was one of the first to introduce this in the courses
of those whom he trained. Glove-rubbing is without

doubt advantageous, but it in no degree approaches to the benefits of proper massage.

Here let me interject a practical tip often overlooked by athletes and trainers. A man should always be dried down well with a towel before the rubbing gloves are used.

The great fault of glove-rubbing is that it is apt to irritate the skin, and I have seen men rubbed quite raw with the gloves.

American Successes.

American athletes are picking up prizes and breaking records all over the world. Why? I attribute these American successes more to the fact that massage takes its correct place in their training—as together with walking exercise the most important item—than to anything else.

Its Objects.

The great object of massage is to loosen the muscles. This makes a man quick, an attribute as necessary in a long-distance man as in a sprinter, only made use of in a less apparent manner.

When I have " been over " a man after he has had a spin, I give him from twenty minutes to half-an-hour's massage, for I find that to thoroughly get at every muscle from head to foot requires to do it comfortably just about half-an-hour.

Removes Bad Flesh.

At the commencement of training there is nothing like it for removing every ounce of bad flesh, and encouraging muscle development of a right sort.

For Rheumatics

The man who is regularly massaged will never grow muscle bound, a failing of far more otherwise magnificently developed men than would be generally credited.

A Great Boxer's Opinion on Suppleness of Muscle.

Robert Fitz-Simmons, the boxer, has something very strong to say on the subject, in a special chapter on non-supple muscular development, in his excellent book, "Physical Culture and Self-defence," [1] but, strange to say, he has no word as to the best of all remedies—massage.

For Rheumatics.

Quite apart from strict training purposes, massage is, I consider, one of the finest health-givers and preservers known to man.

As a cure for those who suffer from Rheumatism, commend me to a systematic massaging after a warm bath, and I think you may then throw all doctor's physic down the sink. The massage will literally push the disease out of the body.

It may be thought that I speak too strongly, but experience impels me so to do. The difference I have seen it work in one man after another, never failing to act as a fine tonic to the whole system, makes me feel that even at the cost of repeating myself I must urge the practice, as an absolute necessity to the man who would bring himself to the highest pitch of bodily

[1] "Physical Culture and Self-defence," by Robert Fitz-Simmons, published by Messrs. Gale & Polden, Amen Corner, London, E.C.

perfection, and as of utmost benefit to almost all people.

How to do it.

It is of course best to be massaged by some one else, but there is nothing to prevent a man from massaging himself.

To do so, commence rubbing the chest with one hand and the back with the other, with an upward circular motion. Whilst the right hand rubs the left side of chest, the left hand rubs the right shoulder blade, and *vice versâ*. In these positions of the arms one can work all over the body, back and front, from the neck down to the top of the thighs. Do not miss a spot. Rub softly and briskly. Between the rubbing, catch hold of pieces of your flesh and muscle between the first finger and thumb, and lightly squeeze them. It is this pinching which is the principal part of my system. Great care must be exercised not to cause bruises.

This pinching also gets rid of the bad flesh, softens the muscle, and allows it to develop just as it should.

Let each hand run over in like fashion the opposite arm, giving the biceps a specially lively pinching. Next pinch the muscles quickly all over the thighs back and front from the knees to the groin. One hand can take each thigh and then work from the calves downwards to the ankles and all over the feet.

To obtain the full benefit, the subject should during massage relax each muscle which is being touched, and in this lies the advantage of having some one else to do it for you, as it is much easier to relax your muscles when lying inactive, than when you yourself are doing the work, for this in itself is a fairly tiring form of exercise.

To Develop Special Muscles.

Only actual experience will teach a man to find the muscles all over the body which most require loosening, but after a while one can get at almost every muscle in the frame in this way.

For boxing, special attention to the arm and chest muscles is needed. A fine supple muscular development all over the front of chest and stomach is an invaluable equipment of the boxer.

Cyclists, runners, jumpers and rowing men should pay particular regard to the muscle just over the knee on the inner side of the leg.

After Exercise.

When in training, upon coming into the dressing-room, the best plan is to strip, wipe down with a soft towel (always treat the body with the utmost gentleness after exertion), and lie for a minute or two covered with a couple of blankets, until a more or less free perspiration is induced. Wipe down once more, and then massage. The older an athlete grows, the more benefit will he feel from this.

The Face.

I do not as a rule treat the head or face in this way, but there is no harm in massaging the face'; and for women whose beauty is a consideration there is no weapon so suited to combat the ravishes of time as massage.

CHAPTER III

Sleep, Bathing, and Medicine

Nine hours for sleep—Importance of regularity—People who cannot sleep—Bathing—The morning tub—Warm bath best—An unhealthy practice—Hot sea baths—Medicine —When to take it—Keep bowels open.

THE time of rest and natural recuperation must of necessity vary to suit individual habits, occupations, and a variety of other factors.

I have heard it said, "Seven hours for a man; eight for a woman, and nine for a fool." I disagree entirely.

Nine Hours for Sleep.

To enjoy the best of health, and obtain physical perfection, most people need the "fool's" portion, *i.e.* about nine hours. From 10 P.M. to 7 A.M. is the sleeping time of men I train, and they find it none too much. In fact when in hard training many men during the resting time after the midday dinner drop off into a nap, and so add another hour without any disadvantage.

The number of hours to be devoted to sleep is not more important than the regularity of retiring and rising. Hence a man in training must eschew all evening pleasures which would keep him up after 10 o'clock or thereabouts. Sleep must also be un-interrupted to be of utmost benefit. The general effect of the whole system of training is to encourage sound unbroken rest.

On the day of a race, or other event, the athlete should be allowed an extra hour between the sheets. In cases where a journey has to be made to the place of contest, many first-rate runners put in an hour or so in bed immediately upon arrival at their destination, even though they reach it perhaps only two or three hours before the race.

Importance of Regularity.

Some men, and the number is not a few, chafe against what they consider a boyish restriction, *i.e.* the turning in regularly at 10 o'clock. On the other hand, I can confidently assert that more men have lost their events through neglecting this than from any other single cause.

People who cannot Sleep.

In everyday life very many people declare they cannot sleep so long or so early, or that if they do go to bed at ten and sleep, then they wake in the night. Very likely; but I would inform such that it is because they are not in really good health, and I would undertake that after a month's properly regu-lated life, and proper exercise, they would sleep as soundly as possible for nine hours or thereabouts at a stretch.

The Morning Tub

Bathing.

Opinions on bathing as an aid to training differ considerably. I am not very strongly in favour of much of bathing, and I do not believe in swimming as a rule when training, for cold water stiffens the limbs.

The Morning Tub.

Many people put great faith in an early-morning cold-water dip, and will even go to the extent of breaking the ice in order to get it, but I look upon this as a dangerous practice, and one which should be very much discouraged. To plunge suddenly into cold water produces a shock, the evil consequences of which cannot be over-estimated. And even swimming in cold water at any time, although it gives strength and makes the muscles hard, is not advisable for any one who is training to become an athlete. A morning wash all over from a basin of cold water I do recommend. This is quite a different thing from a bath, and gives neither the shock nor subsequent stiffness.

Warm Bath Best.

A warm (not hot) bath, say twice a week, is excellent.

After a big effort there is nothing which will restore nature more quickly than a warm bath. At such a time the water should be rather hotter than for the ordinary warm bath, and the man should get into it as soon after the finish of his event as possible. The more done up he is the greater will be the comfort and benefit derived.

28

Hot Sea Baths

An Unhealthy Practice.

Here I would like most emphatically to deprecate a custom which prevails at most athletic sports. Attached to the dressing-room is usually a bath which is run nearly full of cold water. Competitors come in one after another after their events, and plunge into it, without the water being changed! Thus perhaps twenty or thirty perspiring men go into the same water. Apart from the injury to the system of a cold water shock at such a time, the unhealthiness of washing in a bath, when one's pores are working especially freely, the water in which contains all the impurities carried off by twenty other men's perspiration seems to me appalling. Needless to say, no man trained by me ever practises this folly.

It would, I am quite aware, need a very rich club to provide accommodation for each man to have a fresh warm bath, so I advise no bath, but that the men should lie under rugs to perspire for a few moments and then have a rub down or massage.

Hot Sea Baths.

A little sea bathing is beneficial. Warm sea-water baths are most invigorating. I used for about four years to go to Brighton from Saturday to Monday more for hot sea baths than anything else.

For those who live in inland towns I can strongly recommend a sponge down first thing in the morning, with Tidman's sea salt in the water. It is an excellent substitute for the real thing.

Medicine.

The healthy man should, in my opinion, not require medicine more than twice a year.

Spring is the proper time for an aperient, and this fits in well with most men's training, for an aperient should only be taken at the commencement, and the majority begin to train in early spring.

The following is my prescription—

Salts, 2 oz.

Senna leaves, ½ oz.

Spanish liquorice, a piece the size of a haricot bean.

Ginger, half a small teaspoonful.

Put the senna leaves, liquorice, and ginger into a tea-pot or other suitable covered jar, and pour half-a-pint of boiling water over them, and allow to stand till the next day, when the salts are stirred well into the mixture till thoroughly dissolved. Drain off the liquid and take a wineglassful as a dose. This should give about four free openings, commencing about two hours after taking it.

When to take it.

The best time to take this dose is first thing in the morning. If a good hot cup of tea or coffee be taken a quarter of an hour later, it will accelerate the action upon the bowels and prevent any griping pains.

If the bowels are at all obstinate, and a thorough clear out is not effected by the first dose, miss a day and then take another wineglassful, which is almost sure to prove sufficient.

Keep Bowels Open

For the rest of the year apples in the mornings after exercise, and plenty of stewed fruit at dinner are the best of all medicaments.

Keep Bowels Open.

To be in good health the motion should be perfectly regular once a day. After breakfast is the best time. This regularity is a matter in which determination of the subject plays a most important part. If one has a more frequent desire than once a day, it must not be restrained; but the addition of a little more rice pudding, and a cutting down of the quantity of stewed fruit, will generally correct this quite automatically.

CHAPTER IV

Food, Drink, and Smoking

*What to eat — Avoid experiments — Meals — Breakfast —
Dinner — Tea — Between meals — Plasmon — Drink
— Teetotalism — Moderate drinkers — Abstainers —
Smoking.*

What to Eat.

WHAT people should eat is a subject which has lately,
at any rate in the athletic world, been the most discussed of all questions.

No-breakfasters, vegetarians, fruit-eaters, and many
more have each and all aired view after view of the
subject, with varying degrees of confidence and per-
sistence.

My experience as a practical man leaves me no room
for doubt upon this subject. I have seen men trying
one or other of all the various systems, and have only
become more and more convinced that an ordinary
everyday plain meat diet is far superior to all nut-
eating or fasting plans.

Avoid Experiments.

That clever writer, Mr. Eustace Miles, has kept well
to the forefront in the laying of new diet projects before
the reading public; but I must say that the uncertain
tone with which he introduces some of the schemes

is to my mind a sufficient evidence that he himself is not thoroughly convinced that they are really advisable. Further, I cannot see that the suggestions thrown out for people to try these unproved systems can do anything but harm. I am, however, digressing, and return at once to a plan of diet that I have no hesitation in recommending to every healthy person. Those who are not possessed of average good health can hardly hope to become athletes, hence my suggestions throughout this book assume the reader to be blessed with at least a fair share of this prime blessing.

So much is made of the "one man's meat another man's poison" side of the diet question that I should like to say that, so far as athletes are concerned, I have always found very little in this saying, and I am constrained to believe its almost universal acceptance as a truth is more due to its triteness than to its truth.

Meals.

A man in anything like a fair state of health will thrive, and, if other points allow, will reach a state of extreme fitness, on a simple diet such as follows :—

Three meals a day are, I consider, necessary. Breakfast, dinner, tea. Exact times need not be laid down ; but breakfast at about 8.30, dinner at 1, and tea from 5.30 to 6 o'clock are suitable hours.

For a man in training I give as follows :—

BREAKFAST.—A couple of new-laid eggs and toast,

followed by a little cress or marmalade, or both ; or half-pound of fresh fish and toast, cress or marmalade, or both.

A steak or a chop may sometimes take the place of the eggs or fish.

I disallow bacon and butter, only occasionally permitting just a very little butter to a man who may particularly fancy it.

DINNER.—Roast beef, mutton, boiled mutton, poultry, game, milk puddings, and stewed fruits, plenty of green vegetables. As great a variety of food as possible from day to day is advisable. I bar pork, rabbit, hare, venison (this is apt to upset the inside), boiled beef, and potatoes. No suet puddings or pastry. Shell-fish are also taboo, as are all kinds of cheese.

TEA.—Consists of eggs, fish or poultry, toast or crust of bread ; the crumb should always be toasted and the crust eaten stale, not new. Water-cress is allowed, but very little if any butter.

As a general rule, I think it best to let each one regulate the quantities for himself. I find that in the long run they generally level off to about the amounts stated above.

Between Meals.

A biscuit or two, or an apple after the morning exercise, and a biscuit also about 9 o'clock in the evening, in addition to the above meals, complete the solid side of the food question.

Plasmon

Cooking.

The old idea of meat almost or quite raw is a great mistake, as very few people can digest it. It is most important that all food should be well cooked. I do not mean over-cooked, but just as a good cook would serve it.

Plasmon.

As a general principle I am not in favour of what may be roughly described as prepared foods—I mean the general run of proprietary articles, but I am in most hearty accord with Messrs. C. B. Fry and Eustace Miles in recommending that during training, certainly during its earlier stages when nourishment and building up of the body are all-important essentials, no athlete can afford to overlook the benefits to be derived by the addition of Plasmon, wherever possible, to his food.

Plasmon is the nourishing food-substance of pure fresh milk in the form of granulated powder, so prepared that it is practically the most easily assimilable form in which food can be taken into the human frame. Medical men throughout the country recognise the value of Plasmon as a nutritive of great importance. It has the advantage of being conveniently added to almost every kind of food, for it is odourless as well as tasteless. Gravies, soups, and cocoas should always have a teaspoonful added, whereby their nourishing powers are at least trebled and often still further increased.

It is of comparatively recent introduction, but its

effects on the diet of athletes have been almost as astonishing as were those of pneumatic tyres when first applied to cycles.

Like most things in this life, moderation in use must be exercised. To the food mentioned in the three meals a day above described, a total amount of not more than half-a-dozen teaspoonfuls of Plasmon should be added.

Some athletes are beginning to regard Plasmon as an almost complete diet. With this I do not agree, regarding it rather as a most valuable addition to fresh meats, drinks, and other natural foods.

What to Drink.

Whilst I have found athletes and men in training all settle down to a practically uniform diet of solids, on the liquid refreshment question there is, and, I suppose, always will be, a wide divergence of opinion and habit.

Teetotalism.

For myself, I am a teetotaller, and have never known the taste of alcoholic liquor. This came about through my having in childhood had several very forcible object-lessons of the fatal effect of over-indulgence in stimulants, on the part of numerous acquaintances of more mature age than myself.

For this reason I cannot speak from experience on my own body further than to say that I have never felt the need of alcohol, and have been able to train myself into first-rate condition without it.

Teetotalism

Needless to say, I have gone into this point very carefully in the form of observation of others, and my opinion is this: To those unaccustomed to stimulants there is no advantage to be gained by taking them. To those who are not teetotallers there is no advantage, in fact, there is a disadvantage, in knocking them off entirely.

Amongst the men whom I have trained there have been many teetotallers, and many moderate drinkers, for I will not take any man in hand who is not moderate, and upon running through their careers and achievements I find very little difference between them. Some of my best champions have been teetotallers, and others have taken their beer.

The teetotaller has one advantage in that, when out of training, he has no temptation to indulge too freely in alcohol, and so put heat into his blood which will lead him into sensual indulgences more than the non-drinker, and so shorten his career as an athlete.

In justice I am, however, bound to say that amongst my men those who have remained moderate drinkers, out of as well as in training, have lasted quite as long, and in one or two exceptional instances even longer, than most of the teetotallers.

To sum it all up, if you are at present an abstainer, don't start stimulants. If you are a moderate drinker, don't drop it, but be most careful to be just as moderate out of training as in.

Now as to what and when to drink in training. The following are the two systems I prescribe for my men.

Moderate Drinkers.

Let us take first the course which includes stimulants.
Nothing before Breakfast. The cup of tea in bed is very seductive, but must be given up absolutely. At breakfast half to three-quarters of a pint of weak tea or cocoa. At 11.30 to 12 o'clock, after the first exercise and massage, half a pint of old ale or light Burton, and a biscuit. At dinner half a pint of old ale or light Burton. Occasionally, if the man is weak and wants building up, or needs to add a little flesh, I increase him to a pint at dinner on perhaps two days in one week, and after that only the half pint every day. At tea two teacupfuls of weak tea.

In the evening, at 8 to 9 o'clock, half a pint of ale.

From this it will be seen that I allow a man a pint and a half a day, and perhaps on two days early in his training an extra half pint.

Spirits and liqueurs I absolutely bar. Wines are also cut off, with the exception that if a man seems going stale a few days before his event, I give him, after the morning exercise, half a tumblerful of champagne one day in place of the half pint of beer. As will be seen in a later chapter, I find champagne is practically the only wine of genuine use to the athlete.

Abstainers.

I prescribe for abstainers as follows: Nothing before breakfast. Half to three-quarters of a pint of weak tea, cocoa, or chocolate at breakfast. At 11.30 to 12, after exercise and massage, a glass of water or

Smoking

milk and soda, with a biscuit or apple if they want something. I find, however, that the teetotaller rarely wishes for a drink at this time, generally contenting himself with an apple or biscuit, or both.

At dinner half a pint of water or milk and soda-water. At tea, two cupfuls of weak tea. In the evening, between 8 and 9 o'clock, a soda and milk, or cocoa (Plasmon), or chocolate and biscuit.

Ginger-beer and other mineral waters are taken by some men in place of the milk and soda-water. Whilst the majority of these are not harmful, they are also not beneficial, and during training it is best to stick to the actually useful in drink, diet, and habit.

Smoking.

No athlete, I venture to think, will contradict me when I say that smoking is a very great drawback to the man in training. And I will go further than that, and say that while smoking is no good to the ordinary healthy individual, it is rank poison to the athlete.

I know full well that my views on this subject will not be swallowed with such a relish as what I have said under other headings, but though the habit of smoking may be a pleasant one to very many, few, I imagine, will be bold enough to stand up for the weed so far as to assert that it is beneficial to the human constitution.

I have hardly known any smokers who have become champions, and, though I will not make a positive assertion offhand, I may say that I cannot recall, at

Smoking

the time of writing, even one smoking record-breaker. This surely is strong argument in favour of my theory. Ingram, Platt-Betts, Frost, the Bath Road man, Holbein, never smoked in their lives, and to this, in a very great measure, their success is due. I strongly advise any of my readers who are smokers gradually to cut down their indulgence in tobacco to one-half, and they will see how much better they will train.

Robert Fitz-Simmons writes down six rules for young athletes, and two of them are (1) Do not smoke, (2) Do not chew. If you wish to study your health and be strong, do not take tobacco in any form whatever. If you are a regular smoker, and have been so for years, I do not recommend its absolute discontinuance even in strictest training, but a substantial reduction must be made if you intend to do great things, or anything approaching to first-rate feats in any sport.

CHAPTER V

The Athlete's Clothes, and Embrocations

Principal items — Pants — Vest — Sweater — Shoes — Socks — Useful hints — Corks — Boots — Slips — Embrocations — Two kinds — How and when to use them — Strains, Bruises, &c.

Principal items.

CLOTHING for athletics is very much the same in almost all branches. The principal items are shoes, pants, and vest, together with a sweater for use at practice, and to slip on after an event.

All these, except the sweater, are made as loose and light as possible.

Warmth, however, is most necessary, for it gives elasticity to the limbs and body, so on days which are cold and windy I always see that my men wear their long drawers down to the ankle and the short pants over them at practice.

For runners the pants should be very baggy, and loose above the knee, and made of light material, such as merino or silk, though the latter is, I warn readers, rather apt to split. The right things can be obtained

41

Shoes

at Gamage's, High Holborn, London, or at any athletic outfitter's. There is generally one firm in every town of any size which makes a speciality of athletes' requisites.

Shoes.

There are several styles of shoes—ordinary running shoes, rubbers, and bar shoes.

The running shoe is the most useful all-round article. It is a tight, light leather shoe with spikes in the bottom. The number of spikes should be varied according to the weight of the man, and the use they are to be put to.

The following are average :—

> Sprinters, 6 spikes.
> Long-distance track running, 5 spikes.
> Cross-country, 5 or 6 spikes.
> Jumping, 7 spikes, the extra one being in the heel.

Rubbers are all right for running on a hard road, but no good across country or on the track. The cross-country runner's shoe must have a metal plate let in between the leathers of the sole to prevent the spike heads working through and so injuring the sole of the foot.

Bar shoes are no good for any sport that I know of.

Socks.

A runner or walker should wear special socks, made with the toes and front part of sock up to the instep of wash leather. These cost about 1s. a pair.

Useful Hints

Useful hints.

Here I will give a good tip, which I have not seen published anywhere. For walking or running long distances, Russian tallow or pure yellow soap rubbed on the inside of ordinary wool socks all over the foot and ankle part, is a great preventative of chafing and footsoreness. Under and round the crutch of the legs and under the armpits should be well rubbed with the same substance.

Put your shoes on in the dressing-room, leaving them unlaced. Walk thus to the starting-point and then fasten them up at the last moment before the start.

An athlete, particularly a cross-country man, should be very careful of the condition of his shoes. Immediately after a race or run they should be brushed. If they are wet from rain or perspiration, they should be greased.

To keep them from stretching too long, the backs should be bent over forwards, so as to lie right flat upon the heel.

Corks.

Some men carry circular pieces of cork just about as long as the hand is broad and about $1\frac{1}{4}$ inches in diameter. The gripping of them during a run calls for an exertion of will-power which is most beneficial in any feat of strength or endurance. Gamage supplies these at about 6d. or 9d. a pair.

Embrocations

Boots.

As walking forms so regular and important a part of all training, it is essential that well-fitting boots, which give to the foot full room and comfort, be worn. I have personally done a vast amount of walking with men I have trained, and I find a broad-toed boot far better than a round-toed one. If possible, good quality boots should be bought. I pay a guinea a pair for mine, and consider it none too much to ensure comfort in this matter. Whatever the reader does, let him be sure to have a broad-toed boot.

Slips.

Every athlete should wear these as a preventive of the risk of rupture. They are of help in several ways.

Embrocations.

Embrocations play no small part in the rubbing-down and massage of athletes. Very few dispense with the use of them. They are of great assistance in massage to the rubber, quite apart from the good done to the subject.

Two kinds.

There are practically two kinds of embrocation. In the one spirit is the principal ingredient, and in the other oil. Each has its own advantages.

That made with oil is, for general purposes, the best, as that in which spirit predominates dries up too

Strains, Bruises, &c.

quickly as one rubs, and is also very cold. I have seen men, after practice, have it used on them, and shortly afterwards turn icy cold. However, there are times when the spirit embrocation is best.

How and when to use them.

Whenever massage or rubbing down before or after practice is undergone, a little oil embrocation should be used. It should be applied and rubbed in more particularly in the neighbourhood of the muscles which are specially to bear, or have just borne, the brunt of the exercise.

In the event of finding oneself after other exertion wet through, and at such a place that a change of clothing is not possible, a little spirit embrocation poured into one's boots will go a long way to prevent catching a chill on the journey home.

Some athletes regularly use plain methylated spirit to rub with, but I think it does more harm than good, and personally I find George's (No. 1), or Spirit Recordine, for a spirit liniment, and Sandow's Embrocation for an oil lubricant, the best.

Strains, Bruises, &c.

If you are so unfortunate as to strain a muscle of the thigh or calf, or in fact any muscle, or if you come by a bruise, rest immediately—don't attempt to run it off. Have a day or two quite free from exercise, and rub the injured part frequently with spirit embrocation, and hold the limb under a cold-water tap as long as you can bear it, and as often as is possible.

CHAPTER VI

Judging Distance, and Style in Running

*Lack of judgment—How a trainer judges a man's distance
—Self-judging—Style in running—A common error—
Measurement of stride—The sprinting style.*

Lack of Judgment.

RIGHT throughout my career as a trainer, there is no failing that I have so often had brought to my notice as the lack of judgment shown by walkers, cyclists, and runners, as to their "distance"—that is to say, as to the distance at which they are most likely to acquit themselves with success.

Many a good amateur, and many a professional too, has run for years before finding his distance, and in numerous instances, startling as it may sound, they have never discovered this all-important piece of knowledge at all.

In nine cases out of ten, I find that the men who put themselves under me have a quite erroneous idea of the distance they are most fitted to negotiate.

A man starts on a track fancying he is cut out for a sprinter, and sticks to short work without ever trying his powers at anything else, until one day it

Lack of Judgment

comes to him either of himself or through a hint from some good judge of form who happens to see him at work, that longer journeys would suit him better. It is possible that by the time he acquires this knowledge he has so much accustomed himself to sprinting that habit proves an almost insuperable bar to his shining at what should have been his best distance.

Very many cases have come before me of men who have been running for a year as mediocre sprinters, when quite by chance they have run a longer distance, and have discovered that it is their correct line.

How a Trainer Judges a Man's Distance.

Every first-rate trainer, in taking a novice in hand, would make it an earliest point to watch him at runs well within his speed, and from his stride, action, &c., judge his most likely distance at once. Then by clocking him over this distance a few times, and also taking his time over several other journeys, the trainer can confirm or alter his first opinion.

This timing is generally found to bear out the trainer's judgment if he is a competent man, though, of course, some men, whilst in other ways no better trainers than the rest, are specially gifted in this particular point of judgment.

Self-Judging.

It is very difficult for a man to judge his own distance. If he runs alone it is almost impossible to tell, and only good fortune can help him to a correct

Style in Running

decision. To such as have not the advantage of an experienced trainer's help in this matter, my advice is, run with others at various distances, and judge how you hold your own against those of them who seem best at each particular course, and also run yourself against the clock a few times at such distances as the above trials lead you to believe are your best.

If you find you can run a good mile, you can probably go five, or even ten.

The hardest distances to judge one's fitness for are those under the half mile. A good sprinter can never last a mile even at second-rate speed; so if you can do a decent mile, do not sprint, even if at first you seem to go better at the shorter journeys. This may be taken as an invariable rule. There are so few exceptions to it that they may safely be disregarded by any of my readers who are searching for their distance.

A case in point which may interest my readers is that of Mr. Lionel Martin, who rode as a cyclist for some four years on the track, and has now at the end of that time only just found his proper place as a long-distance road man. His Land's End to London record will be known to most cyclists.

Style in Running.

Far more depends upon style in running than would appear to a casual observer. The object of all styles is to propel the runner forward with as small an amount of lifting work as possible. Hence, as a general rule, the runner should steal over the

Measurement of Stride

ground rather than bound along. And now comes a seeming paradox. The longer the stride the better, but one must never try to take long strides. To over-stride oneself is the worst of all faults in running, and it is certain to happen if the runner attempts to lengthen his stride.

A Common Error.

In one of the best known books on training the reader is frequently advised gradually to increase the length of stride and pace till the tape is reached, or it is put in other words to the same effect. If this has been followed by the readers, their chances must have been most seriously injured thereby. All that the athlete must do is to quicken the pace at his *natural* stride.

If a proper course of training is followed, this natural length of stride will be considerably greater when running at full speed after a few months' practice than at the commencement of training.

Measurement of Stride.

Every runner should measure his strides about twice a week. In doing this two strides should always be taken at each spot where a measurement is made, for the length of a stride made with the left foot forward varies from one with the right foot foremost. It is well to take the measurement at two or three points in a run, as this will show whether an even length is being maintained.

The Sprinting Style

The Sprinting Style.

The sprinting style of running may be termed the hardest of all, for to be a success a man must be a naturally good runner, as well as one cultivating correct style. Not too long a stride is required; the main point being to pick up the feet quickly, and carry them along low.

In taking the rear foot up from the ground there is a slight backward throw of the foot. This must be reduced to a minimum. The knees must never be raised higher than the hip. The hands should be alternately worked backwards and forwards, but never brought more than an inch or two above the hips. A frequent fault with sprinters is to work the hands up and down right up to the level of the chin. This fighting-the-air method is really a hindrance, whilst a quick low swing at the hip level is a wonderful help to covering the ground speedily.

The body should be inclined slightly forward and steady. If allowed to sway about it impedes one's progress.

Do not throw the head back, and do not look into the sky. Let the head be poised at the same slightly forward angle as the body, and in short sprints look straight for the tape. In longer sprints it is perhaps as well to keep an eye upon the heels of a competitor just in front until you make your supreme effort and dash to the front at the finish. In this way your rival becomes an unconscious pacemaker. Should he be passed, you must, of course, keep close on to the man who has forged ahead.

CHAPTER VII

The Start and the Finish

Starts and starting—All-fours start good for the over-anxious — Its disadvantages — Forcing the finish — Champagne the best stimulant—Drugs dangerous.

Starts and Starting.

IN all sprint races, although much depends upon speed, very much also depends upon the start. That a good start in a short race, which is invariably won by inches only, should be made, must be apparent. Runners for sprints have different pet methods of "getting out of the hole."

The two principal are known as the "Dab" start, which is favoured by Hutchens (an illustration of which is given on the cover of this book), and the "Hand-spring" or "All-fours" start, which A. R. Downer prefers. For the dab start the runner places one foot, usually the left, with toe on the mark, while the toe of the other foot rests in a small hole, which the runner makes with the spikes of the shoe, some eighteen inches behind. When the pistol is fired, the runner makes a little forward dab with the front foot, and instantly swings himself forward into full pace.

For the hand-spring start, the man goes on all-fours,

the tips of his fingers touching the mark, the toe of the front foot about six inches behind the mark. He by that means gets some push off with his hands and a very powerful push with back foot.

Another curious method of starting is that adopted by the well-known sprinter, Cross, who has the right hand on the ground and the left up.

There are other well-known runners who show some little peculiarity in their way of getting off, and it is quite a moot point as to which method is the best in order that some advantage, however slight, may be secured. Personally, all things considered, I prefer the dab start. The all-four idea was first brought from America, and it was introduced in order to cheat the pistol, as the man who adopted this method could see the smoke before he heard the report. That was when starters fired the pistol downwards behind their back; but many of them now fire in the air, so that the all-fours starter does not get this advantage. Some starters even now keep to the old style of firing downwards, and where this happens a hand-starter invariably gets off first. If they gain half a yard or a yard it is a lot in a sprint.

All-fours Start good for the Over-anxious.

Another advantage is in the matter of steadiness at the start. There is no doubt that the all-fours starter, if a nervous man (and some of the best are the most nervous), is less likely in his excitement, when the starter calls "set," to get over his mark before the pistol is fired, thereby incurring a set-back of one yard.

Its Disadvantages

Its Disadvantages.

On the other hand it has a couple of most serious disadvantages. First, the runner must have his front foot quite six inches behind the mark, so giving the dab starter six inches—more than many a sprint is won by, bear in mind. Then there is the raising of the body to an upright position, in itself an effort equal, I should say, to quite a tenth of a second, or one whole yard at the end of the race. Again, this method involves a very great strain on the muscles of the back of the thigh, and has frequently caused a break-down, so that it cannot be practised often in training for fear of such a calamity. Should a strain be come by, knock off work at once and rest, treating the part with embrocation and cold water as described in the chapter on Embrocations.

A man should never in starting have to screw round, because it is very dangerous, and lots of men lose races by it. Those who funk invariably look round, and it is one of the greatest mistakes possible. An error made at the start may cost a man a couple of yards, and that in a sprint can hardly ever be made up. The game is to spring off the mark directly the pistol is fired, and get into pace as quickly as possible.

Most of the American sprinters start with the handspring, which, by the way, was introduced into this country by T. L. Nicholas, the great quarter-mile amateur champion of 1890. After a good start, one needs a steady, quick forward motion, and a man should always keep his eye on the tape.

Champagne the Best Stimulant

Forcing the Finish.

At the end of a very long-distance event of either walking, running, or cycling, it is extremely difficult for a man who has been going hard for hours to put in a strong finish.

It is at such a time, if at any, that stimulants may be resorted to. The very fact that he has been kept away from them during training and during the race, will make their temporary effect upon him the more sure.

Champagne the Best Stimulant.

About twenty-five minutes before the finish, half a sponge-cake soaked in champagne, followed five minutes later by a third of a tumblerful of the wine, will, I consider, enable a man to get every ounce out of himself, as the sporting phrase has it.

A new-laid egg beaten in brandy is preferred by some, but this must not be taken more than twenty minutes before the end, for its effect is over in that time.

A mistake made in the giving of either of these stimulants ten minutes too soon might lose a man the successful result of a long training and an exhausting sustained effort, so I need hardly further emphasise the necessity of not giving them too soon.

Drugs Dangerous.

Drugs are used for this purpose by American athletes, but I do not believe in them. I regard them as dangerous, and injurious to a man's future fitness.

CHAPTER VIII

Some General Hints

Taking your weight—Don't overdo it early in training—Start steadily—A fine leg exercise—Continence during training.

Taking your Weight.

THE man in training should take his weight at least every other day.

A very celebrated old trainer used to say that there were three tests of a man's fitness—his watch, his weighing-machine, and his looking-glass. The first, used day by day at practice runs, shows how much speed is being gained or lost; the second, by carefully comparing its records with those of the watch, will show a man what is really his best weight to make good times with. Once this is ascertained by averaging the weights on half-a-dozen occasions, when the watch shows the best times, the athlete can always endeavour to keep as near this weight as possible.

The mirror shows the man if his eyes are bright, fresh, and sparkle like those of a healthy child, then he is fit and well. If the glass shows any dulness, or dead-codfish look about them, it is certain he is out of condition, stale, or overdone.

Start Steadily

Don't Overdo it Early in Training.

It is a most easy thing to fall into the serious mistake of overdoing the training in its early stages. The young athlete, or the more experienced one, starts training for an event. The first impulse is a desire to get fit quickly. In fact enthusiasm in what has been undertaken tends to make a man go ahead too fast.

The man who has never trained before will certainly need a somewhat slow process of getting his body into good order to stand severe physical efforts.

The athlete, after he has gone out of training, say in the late autumn, and starts again in early spring, will have made a quantity of useless fat and flesh, which must be quietly disposed of before he can do anything like what he was doing at the end of his last season, though his natural desire is to get quickly into that form and then improve on it.

Start Steadily.

Athletes as a class more commonly suffer in after life from enlarged heart or fatty heart than other people. Now I put this down to an almost universal practice of getting to hard work too quickly instead of taking it very easily at first.

As a general rule the work during the first two weeks should be light, and designed to rid the body of superfluous fat. No trials, or really sharp or straining efforts, should be made. The delicate organism of and around the human heart needs educating up to the unaccustomed pressure, failing which

A Fine Leg Exercise

nature revolts, and heart weakness, fatal to the athlete's ambition, sets in.

A Fine Leg Exercise.

Running up and down stairs is fine exercise. If possible it should be done in the open air. The steps up to the top of a grand stand on a track form a good practising ground; if these are not available, a few runs from the bottom of a house to the top and down again are good.

This is specially useful to sprinters. Harry Hutchens, the fastest sprinter ever known, always made this an important item in his training. The steps must be taken one at a time. This is important, as the stride required to go up or down more than one at a time is unnatural, and injures a man's form on the track, whilst the one step at a time improves it.

Continence during Training.

We may take it for granted that a man requires all the strength of his system if he is to give full value to the efforts he puts forth in any strenuous athletic contest.

Studying the matter from this most important point of view, I have come to the conclusion, based upon long experience, that the married state is not the best for an athlete, and that in all cases continence is essential to success.

When, under my system, every organ of the body is being brought by strict training to the fullest state of health and vigour, there may very probably be a tendency to involuntary losses during sleep.

These losses are so weakening, and so certain to

Pluck

defeat all the trainer's best endeavours, that they must be effectually prevented.

Let me then advise any of my readers who may be troubled with this annoying tendency, to sew a cotton reel on to the centre of the back of their night-shirt or pyjamas. This will cause them to sleep always on their side, and rouse them with timely warning, if they should turn unconsciously upon their back, as is always the case when the discomfort we are guarding against arises. They will thus be able to avert the drain upon their system which they desire to avoid.

This vital subject, which I have handled as delicately as possible, has not, I believe, been treated in any previous text-book upon training.

.Pluck.

It is not always the best-trained man, nor is it invariably the best runner amongst the entrants, who wins a race. There are two elements, both of which have won many men their races who were really second best. Pluck is the first and perhaps more important. Never think you are beaten. If you feel dead-beat, remember the others are feeling just the same, perhaps worse; so force yourself into a spurt. If you are defeated you will finish closer up to the winners, and it may be the fortune of war that your spurt, trying as it is to you, just cracks up the others, and lands you a winner.

Judgment.

Judgment and diplomacy have also landed a large proportion of trophies. In races of half a mile or

When Not to Pass in Running

over, when you do not know the quality of the opposition, as good a plan as any is to work your way gradually in second or third position, and keep to the inner edge of the track. At three-quarters of the distance get nearer to the leaders and make your effort about 150 yards from home. In the course of the race if any one should pass you, close up with them, so retaining the second or third position.

Try to find out the "fighting weight" of the opposition or the best members of it. If there is only one man you fear, ascertain whether he is a stayer, or whether pace is his strong point. If he is a stayer and you have a nice turn of speed, let him make the pace, reserving yourself for the final burst, when your superior pace will win on the run in. If on the other hand you are a stayer, and your opponent a speedy man, you must make the pace as fast as you can right through from the start, so that you may have him worn out before the finish, in which case he will not have a spurt left in him to race home with on the straight.

When not to Pass in Running.

Never attempt to pass a man on a bend, always improve your position on the straight. Say you do pass on a bend, and that the man in front is on the inside berth and you next to him, you must run quite three extra yards; should you be third man you would run five or six yards extra, and so on.

CHAPTER IX

Sprinting and the Quarter-mile

Sprinting—A light training—The hole—Train with a faster man—Weight—The quarter-mile.

Sprinting.

A SPRINT is a race in which the competitors run the whole distance at the fastest speed they can command. In sporting parlance, "they run themselves all out from start to finish."

Anything from 50 yards to a quarter of a mile is generally reckoned as sprinting, though many athletes consider that the latter distance should not be so classified, for it is almost certain that a man cannot run at his very highest speed much more than 300 yards. Few can manage that, hence I give the quarter-mile a chapter to itself. The sprinting preparation should extend over at least six weeks, but it is better still if eight or nine weeks can be given.

A Light Training.

The sprinter needs a light training compared with that necessary for longer distances. An average day's routine should be: a mile before breakfast—not fast walking—say, just stroll to shop to fetch morning paper, and back to breakfast. Take plenty of time

The Hole

over this meal, and then stroll easily another couple of miles, ending up at the track. Arrived here, go to dressing-room, strip, and massage. Then on to the track and stride out 50 or 60 yards just as a chest-opener.

The Hole.

One should sprint twice or three times out of the hole. To the uninitiated I may explain what the hole is. It is an indentation made in the turf by the runner in which he can plant his back foot at the start, in order to have firm foothold. The hole is usually kicked out with the shoe spikes, though I have seen men scoop it out with a knife. It should be large enough to prevent a slip, otherwise the man may be injured by a strain. A man should start training with three 40's or 50's and then stride through the 100 or 120; commencing at half speed, he should finish fast. When sprinting, one should never pull up dead, but always taper out to a standstill. To pull up dead would soon cause a man to break down. In training for sprints out of the hole always be started by the pistol report, and, if possible, run with others. The worsted should also be stretched across the track when running each of these practice distances. If the sprinter has no trainer, any one on the ground may be asked to fire the pistol for the starts.

Train with a Faster Man.

It is very desirable that the man, or one of them, whom one practises with should be faster than oneself. If no one with this qualification is available, then one of the others should be set with a start of a yard or two, or a few yards, as it is only in this way that one's full speed can be drawn out.

In the early days of training slightly less work for a couple of weeks is all that should be undertaken; speed will come with slow training.

Immediately after these exercises the runner should come into the dressing-room and lie for a minute or two under a rug, and then have another massaging. Walk slowly home to dinner, after which meal take an hour's rest. Once more stroll to track; there is no harm in this walk being lengthened by a détour to make it up to two miles. Undress, massage, and proceed to similar runs as before dinner; massage at conclusion, and home to tea. After tea another stroll for two or three miles.

Many men wear a sweater while at practice. I do not think this wise, at any rate not after the first fortnight. A dressing-gown laid in a handy position and slipped round one whilst standing for a minute or two between the bursts is the best thing. An old overcoat serves the purpose admirably. A trial of the actual distance being trained for should be run once a week against the watch.

Weight.

It does not so much matter to the sprinter if he has a little extra weight to carry, as he has not very far to take it, so it will be found in average cases that the above routine will knock off anything from 5 to 12 lbs. during the first fortnight, after which a slight increase will take place, so that by the day of the event perhaps 3 or 4 lbs. of this will have been regained.

The Quarter-Mile

As a general rule big men make better sprinters than small ones.

The Quarter-Mile.

The 440 yards is the very hardest of all races. Though a man cannot maintain his very highest speed for this distance, yet he must run it as hard as he can from start to finish with no easy.

The training is similar to that for sprinting but must be slightly stiffer. The practice runs must include some of 500 to 600 yards at a moderate rate, to get staying power, and speed must be acquired by several bursts of 40 to 60 yards, and the other distances, as for sprinting. A trial should be run against the watch once every ten days; not oftener.

I have seen many suggestions as to how to run the race to best advantage, but really there is nothing to be said on this point, as there is no time for easing or nursing oneself in the quarter-mile; it is "bat and bat," as we runners say, all the way.

It is a practice of large numbers of runners, and sometimes even of the best, to break at the finish into a gallop home. Do not be persuaded to do this; sprint right through in your natural stride—there is a temptation to break into a longer stride, I know; but resist it, and you will reach the worsted at least a yard or two sooner than if the impulse were given way to.

Amongst first-rate runners the time for a quarter-mile is close round about 50 seconds, but the record stands at $48\frac{1}{4}$ seconds. R. Buttery accomplished this performance at Gateshead on 4th October 1873.

The Quarter-Mile

There are very many sprinters who cannot stay the quarter-mile; therefore it is important that men in training should ascertain as soon as possible exactly what they are fitted for. It is sheer waste of time for a man who wants to win races to keep on training for distances which he will never be able to stay, and he would be more profitably employed in devoting that time to shorter distances. How to find one's distance is explained in another chapter.

CHAPTER X

The Half-Mile, Middle Distance, and Mile

Hard training—Massage—The routine—Never look round — The mile — All-round athlete's distance — Frequent racing—The average time—The record mile.

THE middle distance is anything between the half and three-quarter mile. Races between these distances are far less frequent than at most other distances.

The half-mile requires some staying powers, hence a distinctly harder training is necessary than for the sprint distances. Also no extra weight must be carried, so that the routine which follows is designed to get a man down to his best weight and keep him there.

Before and after both morning and afternoon exercise comes massage, and bear in mind that the after-exercise massage must be preceded by a few minutes' rest under a couple of rugs.

The Routine.

The after-breakfast walk should be about three miles, finishing at track. For the first fortnight run at three-quarter speed a mile or two miles, and in the afternoon walk a couple of miles on the way to the track, and then run three-quarters of a mile at nearly top speed. The evening walk may be from three to five miles. At the end of two weeks change the morning run to 300 to 600 yards fast (one day do 300, the next 600, the next 400, and so on). In the afternoon stick to the three-quarter mile run. During the fourth and subsequent weeks run both morning and afternoon 300 to 600 yards at best speed, and a trial over the half-mile once a week. The exercise the day before the trial should be light.

A half-mile man, when once he has shed all superfluous fat during the first fortnight, should not add weight like the sprinter. If the scales show that he is doing so, the exercise runs must be made a little more severe, and a mile or two more walking added to the routine. For distances over the half-mile and not over the three-quarters, the training is the same, with a proportionate lengthening of the runs according to the distance being trained for.

In the race itself the last two or three hundred yards are the most important. It is no good starting with a rush if you cannot do the finish at a good pace, because those who are behind you at the three-quarter mark would have their opportunity, if they were fit for the whole distance. Never mind if you are going second for the first three parts of the race so long as you are close on the front man and have the staying power. After that you should attempt for all you are worth to take the front position, and when you have taken it be sure you keep it.

Never Look Round.

Don't look back; it is almost certain failure if you do, unless, of course, you have a good lead. But even then it is a great mistake, because, although you may

The Mile

win that particular race, the same act on your part in another race may be the cause of your losing. If, on the other hand, you are racing behind another man who looks behind him, take advantage of it, put on a spurt, and the chances are that you will win. No man can run and look back without losing something. Just before a race it is advisable to take things a bit easy, but don't allow yourself to get stale.

The half-mile record is 1 minute 53½ seconds. This was done by F. Hewitt at Sydney, New South Wales, on 21st September 1871. E. C. Bredin covered the same distance in 1 minute 55¾ seconds at Stamford Bridge on 9th August 1897.

The Mile.

For the mile race you should do practically the same work as for the half-mile, only, of course, increasing the distances walked, and also those of the practice spins. On some days you should cover 400 yards at a pretty fast rate; on other days you might do a fast 600, and now and again go still farther. Occasionally, after the first fortnight, go over the whole distance to get staying powers, and have a trial by the watch once in every ten days.

The All-round Athlete's Distance.

To do a mile in competition with others a man must not only be fast but a good stayer also. It is an all-round athlete's distance. I don't believe in too frequent trials, because then they become dangerous.

The Average Time

Frequent Racing.

There are men who are racing two or three times a week without injury. In such cases, of course, they do not want to train so much as others. Men who are racing so often need only on other days stride through their distances; otherwise, and more especially in hot weather, they would get stale very quickly. Some good sharp walks are very beneficial to the man who is training for the mile; they should not be fatiguing walks, but just long enough—say from an hour to an hour and a half.

The Average Time.

A man to be really good for a mile race must be able to do it in 4 minutes 25 seconds; but it is often done in less time than that, so that the time mentioned would not make a safe thing of it from scratch even at small race meetings, where the best men are not in attendance.

To run a mile to best advantage it is advisable to plan a scale of time for each quarter-mile, and work as nearly to it as possible. The first quarter-mile is always the fastest, the second is slower, and the third the slowest of all. The last quarter ought to be the second fastest, but it rarely is so except in the case of a very fine stayer.

I give a specimen plan for a mile to be run in 4 minutes 25 seconds :—

First quarter .	.	.	I minute	3 seconds	
Second quarter	.	.	I ,,	7 ,,	
Third quarter .	.	.	I ,,	9 ,,	
Fourth quarter	.	.	I ,,	6 ,,	

4 minutes 25 seconds

The Record Mile

The Record Mile.

The man who has made the mile record is W. G. George, when he beat W. Cummings at Lillie Bridge on 23rd August 1886. His time was 4 minutes $12\frac{3}{4}$ seconds, and the probability is that this record will never be beaten. The nearest approach to it was 4 minutes $15\frac{1}{5}$ seconds, by G. B. Tincler, at Worcester, Mass., U.S.A., on 27th August 1897.

W. G. George, as well as being excellently trained after he became a professional, was the most gifted natural runner I have ever seen, so that when practically untrained he could beat most men in the pink of condition.

The times George set for himself were as follows :—

First quarter	.			59 seconds
Second quarter	.	.	1 minute	3 ,,
Third quarter	.	.	1 ,,	6 ,,
Fourth quarter	.	.	1 ,,	4 ,,
			4 minutes	12 seconds

What he actually accomplished was remarkably close to his plan :—

First quarter	.	.		$58\frac{1}{2}$ seconds
Second quarter	.	.	1 minute	$3\frac{1}{2}$,,
Third quarter	.	.	1 ,,	$5\frac{3}{4}$,,
Fourth quarter	.	.	1 ,,	5 ,,
			4 minutes	$12\frac{3}{4}$ seconds

CHAPTER XI

Longer Distances

Two, three, four, and five miles—Good constitution essential—Ten and fifteen miles—Begin easily, and gradually increase speed—Walking valuable.

Three, Four, and Five Miles.

THE training for longer distances—two, three, four, and five miles—is carried on under similar rules to those which govern the training for shorter distances, only of course the ground covered is longer in proportion. What must be borne in mind is that a man should train for pace, and not for distance.

The following is a fair average routine training: During the first two weeks each day run about a mile longer distance than you are training for, at about three-quarter speed. That is to say, if your race is two miles, run three at these practices; if five miles, run six during this fortnight. Wear plenty of clothing on these runs so as to get rid of fat, &c.

The following two weeks do faster and shorter practices. Half your distance at your best speed is perhaps as good a journey as any. Wear now only your racing clothes, and one day a week run a fast trial over the exact distance of your race. The day before this trial take things more easily, merely getting out of your clothes into your running ones, and taking a spin to stretch your legs.

Ten and Fifteen Miles

During this training four to six miles road-walking twice a day is a good amount, and faithfully done every day will ensure staying power.

Only Thoroughly Strong People can Become Long-Distance Men.

It requires strength and a dogged determination to become a successful long-distance runner, and regularity is a great thing to be observed in the matter of training. Every man will improve with training, but only those possessed of the above qualifications, and are also blessed with a strong stomach and sound digestive organs, should go in for long-distance work, as it is particularly trying to these parts of the constitution.

Ten and Fifteen Miles.

Races at these distances require exceptional powers of endurance and staying quality.

The training is harder than for any of the previous distances.

Track practice is confined to once a day, and that in the afternoon. For the first week or two about five miles a day will be enough to run. Afterwards gradually increase the distance to seven or eight miles a day, say three times a week.

Begin Easily, and Gradually Increase Speed.

One trial may be run, but not more, and this should be quite a fortnight before the event, as a full speed run at such a distance as fifteen miles takes a good deal out of a man, and quite a week at the very least is needed to get back what is so lost.

Never exceed the distance you are training for in a practice run, if it be ten miles or anything over.

Long-Distance Running

Walking can Scarcely be Overdone.

Any amount of walking should be undertaken daily. A couple of miles before breakfast. After that meal, massage and walk five miles at a fair pace, and on return massage. Another sharp five-mile walk in the evening, with a massage on coming in, will be none too much to produce the requisite staying quality.

A very occasional burst of speed on the track for five hundred yards will do no harm, and be good practice for an unexpected spurt, which is sometimes the finest way of settling an opponent who is running gamely, but appears to be fagged.

Long-Distance Running.

To train for very long distances a great amount of walking must be done, and this should be on the road, as it is more pleasant, less tiring, and much less monotonous than walking round a track. It is necessary to negotiate many miles both of walking and running at a stretch, the distance to be regulated according to the number of miles a man is training for. Sprinters, as a rule, do not go in for long-distance work, as it would unfit them for the short stages. There is nothing like downright solid hard work and persistency for the man who wants to make his mark as a long-distance runner. It is from the ranks of the cross-country men that the long-distance runners come, because the physical training qualifications are similar.

A sound constitution, heart, and stomach are more than ever needed to stand the shaking up and strain involved in running distances over fifteen miles.

Start a Trifle Heavy

The Routine.

For this class of work the quiet steady building-up process of training is most essential.

At first long road-walks, fifteen, twenty, or thirty miles a day, alternate with runs of a like distance on the track, but at the easiest of speeds.

Good solid and plentiful diet together with this for three or four weeks will be the best preparation for the severe effort which the body is being prepared to undergo.

It is not wise to run a trial of these very long distances at all, as the competitor must save himself for the actual race.

Start a Trifle Heavy.

It is better to start a trifle on the heavy side than trained too fine. The fatigue and wear and tear of the run will take a pound or two or more off a man in a race of this length, and were he to have nothing to spare, the effect would be disastrous to his chances.

It is more difficult to lay down hard and fast rules for these long journeys than for the shorter distances, as the difference in the requirements of various men is much greater than in the shorter races.

In the actual race, the time to try to win is when you see your most feared opponent having a bad time. Go ahead then for all you are worth, and endeavour to run the heart out of him, or if he is in too bad a state to challenge your spurt, try to secure such a lead as will be impossible for him to recover, however exhausted you may be by the extra effort.

CHAPTER XII

Cross-Country Running

How to train—The best build—An expert's advice.

How to Train.

TRAINING for cross-country running should be much on the same lines as long-distance track work, though perhaps of a more arduous nature. You must train steadily, carefully. Do very little hard work at first, and gradually increase in the rigour of training. Go out two or three times a week, and, where it is possible, do your training with others. To train alone for cross-country running is too monotonous.

Of course there are many who cannot give up much of their time in the week for this sort of work, owing to their ordinary occupation. My advice to those who are so situated is to walk as much as they can in going to and from their work, and to utilise some part of their meal times in that way.

Cross-country running is different from ordinary track running in that it is heavier work and therefore requires greater staying power. One very important point to be considered in cross-country running is the clothing. Many men make a great mistake in running too lightly clad. It must be remembered that the

The Best Build

running has to be done in the fall of the year, when chilling rains or driving sleet may have to be encountered, and unless proper clothing is worn serious results may follow. Properly spiked and plated cross-country shoes are also a necessity. At the conclusion of a hard run hot liquid should be applied both externally and internally; for the former purpose a hot bath is the thing, and for the latter a cup of hot beef-tea.

The Best Build.

So far as the build of cross-country runners is concerned, the thick-set man of medium height is more likely to hold out than the thin tall one who wins mile races on the track. There are, of course, numerous obstacles to be encountered in cross-country running. As to hedges, it is better to push through them where possible. To jump them takes too much out of you. At least two runs a week should be taken, as a man gets stiff if resting from Saturday to Saturday. There should be plenty of fast work on the road or track.

An Expert's Advice.

One of the best-known cross-country runners and trainers of young cross-country runners is Mr. R. R. Conway, the President of the Cambridge Hare and Hounds, and I cannot do better than quote him on the subject.[1] He says :—

---

[1] " Athletics of To-day," by Harold Graham. Publishers : Ward, Lock & Co., Limited.

An Expert's Advice

"It is a fact not generally recognised that cross-country running is an art of itself, requiring its own method and its own preparation. Of course in a dozen cross-country runners one may see nearly a dozen different styles, but the method employed will be in every case practically the same. A man needs a very keen eye to the natural features of a course, and a very quick insight into the special needs of the moment, if he is to shine in good company on strange ground ; a double contingency which he must inevitably face if he ever wishes to attain any eminence in this branch of sport."

Then he goes on to say :—

"To arrive at the pink of condition for an important cross-country race, a more arduous preparation is certainly necessary than for any distance event on the track. A path runner knows pretty well when he is running up to form by the evidence of the watch, but time test in cross-country running is of little value, except to show the amount of combination arrived at by the members of a team. It is safe to say that no genuine cross-country course is in the same condition for two weeks together ; a day's heavy rain, or two or three frosty nights, may make a difference of twenty seconds a mile, and therefore comparative times are eminently fallacious.

"To be really fit to race, a man must be ready to make any unforeseen exertion at any moment, whether to settle an adversary, or to combat the natural difficulties of hill and dale, or those artificially introduced by the use of the plough. If one possesses pace rather than stamina, it is absolutely necessary to husband it for grass or road ; again, the steady plodder must be prepared occasionally to force himself along a good deal faster than he likes, if he is to avoid defeat in the run in, or in the language of the sporting scribe, ' final dust up.'

" These conditions obviously require a state of perfect bodily condition. . . . The preparation must be gradual, not forced, and no really hard work should be done for at least a fortnight after beginning training."

CHAPTER XIII

Some Practical Points

Sundays off—Pacing—Cycle pacing—Holding the watch—
Where to stand for timing.

Sundays off.

FOR several reasons quite apart from religious ones, I believe in six days being sufficient for the various practices of training, and at any rate a partial rest being indulged in upon the seventh.

A day off after every six is a fine preventative of over-training, and consequent staleness.

There is no reason for the day to be spent in absolute idleness, as it affords an opportunity for a long, pleasant country walk, which will come as a relief to the man in training after the monotony of his daily visits to the track.

There is another practical reason why Sunday must perforce be omitted from the regular routine in the case of most men—the track will, in nine cases out of ten, be closed on this day.

Pacing.

A pacer, as all athletes know, is one who "makes the running" for another. A man who is being paced

Pacing

should always keep his pacer in check; that is to say, if the pacer is going too fast or too slow let him know the fact at once. If you are being paced, always lay up close to your man and keep him going at your own speed. A man should regulate his pacer, human or motor, as he would regulate his watch, and he should always be as exact as he can.

One very important point is, when changing pacers, always to see that you are picked up promptly. To be left even for a moment is bad management. The change should be so timed and arranged that no hitch, even of the slightest character, can occur. One danger of changing is that the new pacer, being fresh, is apt to go too fast. Be careful therefore that you do not let the new man "jump" from you, as that will break a man up more quickly than anything else.

To be well and properly paced is most valuable to a man at his practice, but to be badly paced is no good whatever. There is much more in this than is apparent to most people. When walking, running, or cycling in races, always have the pace made for you by your competitors, unless for reasons of judgment you decide to make the pace hot for them, to wear them down. Pacing in walking or running is worth 30 yards in a mile, and so on in proportion to the distance you are going. Of course it is worth a great deal more in cycling.

If possible always be paced by a man a shade faster than yourself, or make the man so by handicap, so that you may be pulled out to your full extent. Of course pacing is not allowed in actual walking or running races.

Holding the Watch

Cycle Pacing.

Cycle pacing is now-a-days almost confined to motors, and the motor pacer has become quite an expert at his particular calling, who will soon put the man he is pacing up to the requisite knowledge of how to take the greatest advantage of his pacer.

Holding the Watch.

The timing of a race or trial, particularly at the sprint distances, is quite a fine art. I have met very few good clock holders.

For this reason the amateur must not be too certain, because at several trials against time during his training he may have been timed to do very fast performances, nor need he be despondent in the reverse instances. Even the professional clockers make frequent mistakes, so the chances are much against your friend's time being correct.

Where to Stand for Timing.

A fault I have most frequently noticed is that the watch holder, official or amateur alike, stands right up at the edge of the worsted. Now it is my opinion that this makes a correct timing almost impossible.

One should stand in a line with the worsted, from 5 to 10 yards away from the edge of the track or farther.

Then again there is a particular knack in striking a stop watch accurately which is only acquired with years of practice: hence, as many officials of athletic meetings are young and comparatively inexperienced men, they have never had the opportunity of becoming proficient.

CHAPTER XIV

Bad Times

Losing heart—Some instances—The remedy—
Drugs—Cocaine—Strychnine.

Losing Heart.

In all feats requiring protracted endurance there comes to every man what is known to the old hands as a " bad time."

At such an occasion it is all important that the competitor be quickly pulled together.

Bad times take the heart out of the gamest, for the time being. It is vital that your man does not lose heart, and that the period of prostration shall be ended with all possible speed.

Many and widely diverse are the devices resorted to by various men to combat the dead-beat feeling, which the trainer knows will pass off if only his man is given the right thing, and persuaded to stick to his task.

Some Instances.

I have seen such a champion lion-hearted stayer as Montagu Holbein, when making his best world's cycling records, having such a bad time that he could

The Remedy

not get five miles an hour out of his machine. Half-an-hour later he has been merrily bowling along at 20 to 25, apparently not turning a hair.

Recently, on his magnificent walk to Brighton and back in 21 hours 35 minutes, Mr. J. Butler experienced one very bad time, but pluck and the right attention soon dispelled the temporary weakness.

I mention these two instances only to show that every man who undertakes lengthy feats of endurance must be prepared to face and overcome this, for no matter how good a man may be, or how well trained, it will certainly happen to him on one day or other.

The Remedy.

Many pronounce for brandy, or the yolk of a new-laid egg and brandy, as a reviver. If the athlete be within twenty minutes of the finish then this may be permissible, but as a general thing I most strongly condemn the use of brandy as a stimulant for athletes.

If the man be thoroughly fit and properly trained for his special feat, and fed little and often on the journey on beef-tea (the Liebig Company's Oxo will be found the most effective and handy form for quick preparation, an exceedingly important item when the course takes one into out-of-the-way places and every minute occupied is a consideration), rice-pudding, fruit, such as apples, pears (this fruit is, I know, generally looked upon as bad; but I have found pears particularly good for tired walkers or runners), or bananas, according to his fancy, then, when the bad

Drugs

time comes, a cup of hot tea or a very strong cup of Oxo, with the yellow of a new-laid egg beaten in it, will generally be found effective, and set him well going again within ten minutes or a quarter of an hour of his taking it, and should keep him going strong for hours afterwards.

If the trainer finds that the man is really very, very done up, I recommend half a tumbler of champagne. Spirits of any sort will pull him together for twenty minutes or half-an-hour, and then leave him worse than ever, and also make his stomach reject any good solid nourishment which may be subsequently given. Champagne, if not administered too freely, will not have anything like so injurious an after-effect; but I prefer the hot strong Oxo in most cases, reserving the wine for an absolutely last resource, to prevent a complete break-down.

Drugs.

From America, whose citizens are far ahead of us in most matters of training, has come one most injurious practice, namely, the use of drugs as stimulants.

I have tried them on men I have trained, and as a result have no words of condemnation of their use strong enough to express my mind on the subject.

Several doctors, whose opinions I took before even experimenting with them, whilst not absolutely condemning, were yet adverse to their use. However, as I believe in practical experience, I tried them for several men who were personally desirous of seeing what they would do for them.

Cocaine

Cocaine.

Cocaine lozenges are, I believe, mostly resorted to, consequently those were experimented with. I will not mention the name of the champion rider who was the subject of the experiment, but merely give the result. After taking them he seemed fairly maddened and made a magnificent spurt, but in less than half-an-hour it died away, and he was clean played out—just soon enough to stop his breaking a record which I believe would otherwise have been a certainty.

Possibly the Americans are more skilled in how to administer the drugs than we; in fact I feel sure they must be, seeing that they avoid such break-downs as above described. All those whom I have talked to on the subject admit that each time a drug is used, more and more is required, and that the ultimate result is bad.

I think that it may often be due to this cause that American champions, invincible as they seem when at their best, and who certainly are in other ways trained to perfection, rarely last year after year as the pick of our men on this side do.

Strychnine.

Strychnine in lozenge form is also used. I tried this once on a man during a bad time, and it had no effect at all, so I reverted to hot beef-tea, and got my man home all right.

A use of strychnine, which is under certain circumstances wise, is discussed under the chapter on Worry.

CHAPTER XV

Funk and Worry

Anxious moments — The remedy for funk — Influence of worry—Unavoidable distress—Helped by a drug.

Anxious Moments.

IT must not be thought that a competitor who is seized with extreme nervousness or funk prior to his event is necessarily going to be a failure.

It is my experience that all men funk more or less as the important time of contest draws near.

Many of the world's best champions have I known to grow so anxious, that just before a race they actually could not hold their water. So it must not be concluded that because a man is excessively nervous or anxious, he is chicken-hearted. The fact that he is being put on his mettle, that he is going to pit his weight, so to speak, against the others, calls forth a certain amount of anxiety, which is more apparent and more intense in his case than in others.

Although a man may funk just before the race, immediately the pistol goes off he is himself again, and he puts his best leg foremost (to use a well-known phrase) in his effort to win. But to funk on the day of the race, and especially just before the race, is

Influence of Worry

somewhat against a competitor, more particularly at the start of an event. In his anxiety he may get over the mark and be penalised; or, on the other hand, in order to avert such a thing happening, he may make a bad start, and this in a short race is serious.

The Remedy for Funk.

Let me give a word of advice to all who are in attendance on a competitor in a race, for it is with such that the remedy lies. Talk to him about anything else but the race itself; keep his mind occupied, if you can, on some subject which interests him outside the event in which he is about to participate. His chance of winning will be all the better for a little diplomacy of this sort on your part.

Influence of Worry.

One of the worst things for an athlete to suffer from is worry. By this I do not refer to a man who funks winning his race; that matter has been already dealt with. What I mean is that a man may during the time of training have some private trouble, or fancied trouble, over which he broods and worries, and when this is the case he can rarely hope to become thoroughly fit.

I remember hearing on one occasion a well-known member of the Stock Exchange say, "I never look back." What he meant to convey was that the past was over and all the worry in the world would not alter matters. That is how runners and other athletes should take things. Of course there are people who are always in a state of worry, and try all they may they cannot stop. Such a man is no good at racing, and he had better give up all idea of becoming an athlete. I do think, however, that the majority of men who go in for sports are free and easy in their nature, and are not given to unnecessarily worrying over small matters. But I feel it necessary to make these few remarks, for nothing will do more to break down a man than brooding over trouble.

Unavoidable Distress.

Sometimes real trouble comes to a man, and must be borne. The death of a very dear relative or a serious financial embarrassment happens perhaps within two or three weeks of an important event. If the competitor can postpone his effort, it is certainly the wisest thing to do.

There are cases in which postponement is impossible, and then the athlete's chance is poor indeed; for there is practically no cure for such worry, and its effects on the man's powers are simply appalling. There is, as I said, no cure; but the trainer must do all he can to lessen the evil.

Helped by a Drug.

I am, as will be noticed throughout this book, dead against anything in the nature of drugging; but I think it only right to mention a case of great worry during training, where the man was quite unable to get fit, and under the highest medical advice took a drug daily for the last six days with most satisfactory results, and no traceable injurious after-effect.

Helped by a Drug

The event was a long and trying feat of endurance ; the would-be performer of which was a man whose training as a rule gave me but little anxiety. In this particular case he was, all through the training (and had been for months before), harassed with financial troubles, with the result that a week before the all-important day he was thoroughly "off colour," and hence a certain loser.

During these last six days he took a dose of one-sixtieth grain of strychnine three times a day, which so far improved him that he did a wonderful performance.

Should any reader be in like plight, I would not advise him to try this except under his doctor's orders.

CHAPTER XVI

Vital Organs and Shape

*The heart—The lungs—Weak lungs—Breathing exercises
—Shape—Some typical examples—Aim always at
improvement.*

The Heart.

ATHLETES as a class are more subject than other
people to enlarged hearts or fatty degeneration of the
heart. There is no need for this. Athletics should
do all the functions of the body, present and future,
good—not harm. The heart and lungs should be
particularly benefited.

The reason that an enlarged heart has come to be
looked upon as an athlete's necessary penalty for his
sport, is that very few men are properly trained.

The keynote of training is moderation—particularly
in its early stages. The man who begins with easy
work, and limits himself to it, until by means of it
after two or three weeks the body is fit for greater
exertions, will never bring on fatty heart, at the time
of training or after it is ended.

Over-excitement is to be avoided.

Sudden dashing into cold water after sharp exercise
has, next to too hard exercise in the early stages, done
more than anything else to cause heart trouble to be

associated with athletics. I cannot too strongly condemn this practice, which is touched upon in the chapter on Bathing.

The Lungs.

Without the lungs in good condition, and fulfilling their functions freely and amply, no athlete, or for that matter no man or woman, can do themselves justice in any physical exercise.

If the lungs are actually affected by some disease, it is outside my province in this work to advise upon the matter, further than to recommend immediate recourse to a competent medical adviser.

Weak Lungs.

There are, however, very many people, whose lungs without being diseased are decidedly their weak point. When I encounter such an one, I set myself, in the early part of his training, specially to strengthen this weak spot. It is vital that every competitor in any sport should not ignore the old truth that "the strength of a chain is that of its weakest link." I first dose the subject regularly, in addition to his other diet, with Cod-liver Oil, which I have found a most useful lung tonic.

Very light dumb-bell exercise several times a day, following the chart which is given by the Sandow firm with the grip dumb-bells, making use of those exercises which are specially designed to help the lungs, will be found a wonderful lung strengthener. These are pointed out on this chart.

Shape

Breathing Exercises.

Fitz-Simmons recommends a number of breathing exercises, as do the teachers of most systems of modern physical culture. Personally, I consider the points I have mentioned, together with the greatest possible amount of out-door walking exercise, quite sufficient to remedy ordinary weakness of lung-power.

I would again emphasise that some who are weak or have diseased lungs need very special lung exercises and treatment; and until these have been undergone, I would advise such subjects to avoid athletics, except under the advice and direction of their doctor.

Shape.

It is exceedingly interesting to note the varying shapes of different athletes. As a rule a trainer can usually tell at a glance whether a man who comes to him to be put through is likely to do much good, but even trainers sometimes get a surprise by the after performances of the very man they did not expect much from. A good shaped man, generally speaking, makes the best results; but I have seen very poor shaped ones do well.

Among the champions I have known, there have been all shapes. Some had no chest, but good legs. I remember one man who had scarcely any flesh or muscle on him at all: he was merely skin and bones, and yet he could hold all the good ones at his sport. There are many men I have come across who, judging by their chest, would be incapable of winning a race, but their lungs have been all right. Sandow's dumbbell course would in most cases soon bring the chest out, but the exercises would have to be kept up, otherwise it would go back again to the old shape. I have had some very fine shaped ones under me, which, try how I might, I could never get anything out of. A man ought to be good all over alike, and this usually can be got by training.

Some typical Examples.

Montagu Holbein is perhaps as good an all-round man as I have trained. I had him for some time, and we used to walk miles together. He came to me at 14 stone, and when he was fit he was 12 stone 4 lbs. I reduced his weight by putting him on sheer hard work.

Platt-Betts was another one I had under my charge. When I first took him in hand he was a mere stripling, but he developed into a splendid shape. He was a very easy man to train; did everything I told him. After his practice I always took him home, and he was in bed by ten o'clock: he lived regularly. In the second year I had him he beat the one-mile record.

Zimmerman, another champion, was a very good shaped man; he was well proportioned — all over alike.

F. W. Shorland was another I had, but though he had good legs he had no chest; still there was, as every one soon learnt, plenty of stamina in him.

Harry Hutchens, of Putney, the greatest sprinter ever known, was a good shape with a very long thigh, but loosely built.

Aim Always at Improvement

W. G. George, whose mile-running record seems as though it will stand for ever, appeared to have far too little chest-room.

Aim always at Improvement.

I could go on giving different instances to fill several chapters, but think I have written enough to make it clear that no man need think himself incapable of athletic success because he has not a perfect development, or because he is a little too stout or somewhat thin. Every one can improve his weak points if he recognises them, and adds special exercises to his training, calculated to build up the weak parts. Generally speaking, small men have been good for long journeys, and big men for sprinting.

CHAPTER XVII

Valuable Exercises

Garden exercises—Dumb-bells—A good book on
indoor exercises—Value of variety.

Garden Exercises.

THERE should be a free indulgence in garden exercise. I have elsewhere spoken of the importance of skipping, and where one has the opportunity, a bit of digging is advantageous in exercising the muscles. In fact anything of this sort helps a man to train. I have a decided leaning towards all outdoor exercises, if not overdone. At the same time I am a great advocate of indoor exercises, and, further, there are times when one cannot get into the garden, such as on days when it is very wet, or it is inconvenient to go away from home. At such times the value of indoor work is manifest.

Dumb-bells.

One of the most important ways of training indoors is, of course, with the dumb-bells. This kind of exercise should be taken the first thing in the morning, immediately on getting out of bed. I recommend small dumb-bells especially for the beginning of the training;

A Good Book on Indoor Exercises

it will be found that the exertion which they will give will be quite sufficient. Get Sandow's chart which is published at a shilling; it will give you some excellent advice. I can recommend Sandow's grip dumbbells, as will-power has to be exerted in order to hold them, and they are a great improvement on the old-fashioned sort.

Practice at the parallel bars or vaulting bar is good; in fact all sorts of gymnastic exercises should be indulged in moderately.

A Good Book on Indoor Exercises.

There is an excellent book on Home Gymnastics published by Hartvig Nissen,[1] which tells how to train, strengthen, and develop the body, without the use of dumb-bells or other appliances, and I cannot do better than quote from it the following: "Any kind of exercise will put the blood in circulation, cause one to perspire, and even bring the lungs and heart into vigorous action. But that is not exactly what we should take exercise for.

"If a man has a pair of dumb-bells, clubs, wands, chest-weights, &c., he may very well use them, and in some cases they are really of great value. But he must know how to adapt them to his peculiar case. For instance, if one is troubled with constipation, it is not by the use of clubs or wands, but by more especially trunk movements that the relief will come; or, if one

---

[1] "Health Exercises and Home Gymnastics," by Hartvig Nissen, Instructor in Gymnastics at Harvard University and Director of Physical Training at Boston Public School. Published by Ward, Lock & Co., Limited. Price 1s.

Value of Variety

is troubled with insomnia and nervousness, chest-weights and dumb-bells will be of no use; here slow and suiting exercises of the head, trunk, arms, and legs are needed. Or the blood rushes to the head, and some specially adapted exercises of arms and legs must be had to draw it away; or one is 'round-shouldered,' the chest is contracted, and the head and shoulders stoop forward; what is wanted is not to lift heavy weights, but to take exercises which will straighten and strengthen the back and shoulders, and expand the chest."

I have personally no fault to find with these remarks. They are all very well in their way, but I strongly advise the use of small dumb-bells for general training, and especially do I recommend skipping, as it benefits the muscles, more especially those of the legs, and reduces weight quicker than anything I know. It is important not to overdo dumb-bell exercise, for whilst excellent as a supplement to walking, ball-punching, &c., if used to excess it tends to harden muscles which should be kept supple.

Value of Variety.

However, just as with diet, variety of form of exercise is needed; hence I mention all these different methods, not all of them to be practised each day, but all to be brought on different days into the course of training.

CHAPTER XVIII

Cycling and Strenuous Training

*The Cyclist's training—Long distances—Skipping—Not
"child's play"—Putting the weight—Throwing the
hammer—Ball-punching.*

The Cyclist's Training.

A COURSE of training for cycling should be commenced
just after Christmas by taking long rides at half speed
on the roads, when their state permits.   For instance,
each evening up to the beginning of March do ten to
fifteen miles, and at week-ends forty or fifty miles.
After that make a start on the track.   In March it is
very cold, and one should wear long pants and a
sweater, so as to keep as warm as possible.

For the first few weeks do five miles, keeping
to a steady pace, and as time goes on gradually
increase to three-parts speed.   It will not hurt to
do that every night in the week.   Those who
cannot spin out every night, should go as many
nights as possible.   In about three weeks' time
short fast work should follow—say a ride of two
or three miles with about two very fast 250 yard
bursts.   By riding in this way up to Easter you
will get speed, but be careful not to do too many
sprints, as that is very injurious.

The Cyclist's Training

After about a fortnight of the short distance work a man should be fit enough to ride for any race, and this is the time that he should take care of himself and nurse up, especially if he thinks he has got down to his riding weight. By nursing up I mean easing his training somewhat as regards violent exertion. Of course it is difficult to lay down rules for everybody, because everything depends on the man himself.

When a man comes to me I know pretty well what he can do, but I can only lay down general rules for men whom I have never seen, as what would suit one man would not suit another. A man should weigh himself every other day, and if he suddenly drops three or four pounds he may be sure there is something that needs looking into. He may be off his feed, and he must, therefore, get on it again by having one or two days' rest, and an extra half-pint of whatever he drinks for lunch.

In racing always adjust your own machine; go carefully over the nuts to see that there is nothing wanting: it is safer to do this yourself than to trust to others.

Long Distances.

In training for long-distance cycling a man should put in long easy rides on the road, and about twice a week he might do from fifty to 100 miles, and be paced by a tandem or motor. If training for a twelve or twenty-four mile ride, he might start early in the morning— even as early as four o'clock. He could have an egg and milk, or an egg and tea, and then go on for a distance of say seventy miles before he has his breakfast.

Skipping

This sort of training is very good once a week. Holbein used to ride seventy miles before breakfast, and achieved good results by it.

Skipping.

One often hears mothers lament the fact that the skipping-rope is conducive to the increase of the boot and shoe maker's account, but few realise the fact that skipping is splendid exercise, and especially is this the case in training, for it materially helps to develop the muscles, particularly those of the leg. A person in training for a race of any sort, especially for cycling, should not miss this important part of physical culture, and should devote a certain specified time to it every day up to the last week. Regular skipping for a quarter of an hour or twenty minutes is highly beneficial to the athlete. I advise my readers to go in for it. A good plan is to count as you skip. Do 400 or 500 skips for a start, and gradually increase the number in a given time. The monotony may be varied by the variety of steps which can be introduced.

Not "Only Child's Play."

It may sound rather an effeminate form of training, but I can assure any of my readers who take to it that they will not find it "child's play." Many of the best known men introduce this form of exercise into their system of training, and they would just as soon think of going without their dinner as omit the skipping time. As Robert Fitz-Simmons says in his valuable book on "Physical Culture and Self-Defence,"

Putting the Weight

speaking of athletes' practice exercises: "Remember particularly that the number of times you do the exercises is not so important as faithful regularity, and the way in which you do them. Start easily, and gradually increase the number you do of each. You will soon acquire a surprising endurance, as you may easily prove by getting some companion to follow you through the exercises. He may be strong, and perhaps something of an athlete, but unless he is exceptionally well developed he will certainly show signs of fatigue, and may have to stop before you begin to tire."

Michael, nicknamed the Little Welsh Wonder, whose cycling records are legion, always does a thousand skips or so as a leg loosener, before his practice spins upon the track.

Putting the Weight.

This may not be a very interesting kind of sport to on-lookers, but it requires a great deal of strength, and is first-class exercise for the muscles. The weight, usually of iron, should be "put" from the shoulder with one hand, sometimes the right and sometimes the left, so that the exercise shall not be confined to the development of one set of muscles. At the start a man may "put" a farther distance than he will a few days afterwards, but this will be on account of stiffness, which will soon go off if he keeps to the practice regularly.

The feet must be kept within a certain line, otherwise it is not fair practice, and in a competition a step over would disqualify. A man commencing this form

Throwing the Hammer

of exercise will require some little time to get into the knack of balancing well, and until he can do this he will not do much good, but after he has acquired that knack he will go on and improve. Still it is not at all a light pastime or every man's sport—rather the reverse, for it requires a strong athletic man to become a skilled performer.

Excess of practice will do more harm than good, for this hardens the muscles, and makes one slow for other feats.

Throwing the Hammer.

Here is another kind of sport which, like "putting the weight," is not so frequently indulged in as it used to be, but it is splendid muscular exercise. The rules provide that there shall be a nine-foot circle, and that the hammer, which shall not be more than four feet long, shall weigh 16 lbs. The thrower swings hammer and body round together two or three times, and then lets the hammer go. It requires some amount of practice before one can throw the hammer and keep his balance properly, but the way to keep one's equilibrium will come gradually. There is a great knack in letting the hammer loose at the right moment. One should always take care to keep within the circle, as failure to do that at practice would undoubtedly result in similar failure at a competition.

Ball-Punching.

I am a firm believer in ball-punching as an almost indispensable exercise, and entirely agree with A. R. Downer, who, in his book on "Running Recollections

Ball-Punching

and How to Train," [1] says: "Ball-punching is, in my opinion, the finest thing in the world for the wind."

It is one of the least expensive parts of the training programme, which is another reason why so important a thing should not be overlooked. [2]

First get the ball, then hang it up on a level with, or just a trifle lower than, your own head, and instinct will do the rest. Small gloves, just to protect the knuckles, should be worn. Then you may keep on punching as long as you like. You can't have too much of it. You may not prove to be an expert at the start, and you may get a few unwelcome blows as the ball rebounds, but you will soon get used to the art of dodging, and constant practice will make you proficient in less time than you think.

Fitz-Simmons, in writing on ball-punching, or what he calls bag-punching, says: "Practise just as much as you possibly can. That is, first and last, your most important lesson." He is of course writing specially for boxers, but if extra staying power is needed by any athlete, there is nothing like ball-punching, which also generates quickness.

It is not within the scope of this volume to go into the art and practice. It will be sufficient to point out to readers that at almost any gymnasium a lesson or two can be had which will put a man up to sufficient strokes for use as a training exercise.

[1] Published by Messrs. Gale & Polden, Amen Corner, E.C. Price 2s. 6d.

[2] There is a rather general idea that a punching-ball apparatus is expensive. Some are; but one good enough for all training purposes is sold by Health & Strength Co., 29 Stonecutter Street, E.C., for 15s. complete.

CHAPTER XIX

Handicapping and Scale of Penalties

Handicapping and the A.A.A.—Scale of Penalties.

Handicapping and the A.A.A.

AMATEURS who enter for events carried out under A.A.A.—*i.e.* Amateur Athletic Association—rules, and almost all meetings are under the auspices of this wide-reaching association, will discover that they must fill up a form on entry, stating past attempts, successes, &c. The novice will find that he will receive a start known as half-limit. This is midway between scratch and the longest start allowed in the race. For instance, in the hundred yards race the longest handicap, or limit, is ten yards, so the beginner will find himself on the five yards mark (half-limit).

He may be a good man and win. It is not often that this happens at a first attempt; but, if it does, a penalty is incurred, which means that the next time he runs his start will be cut down by a yard, and should he again win, another yard is knocked off, and so on until he finds himself on scratch. After this no further penalty is incurred by winning.

Scale of Penalties.

The following is the scale of penalties for winning distances as published by the A.A.A.

Scale of Penalties

SCALE OF PENALTIES.

For Wins (First Prizes) in Open Flat Handicaps; during the four days following such wins (Sunday not included).

"No person other than the Handicapper shall be permitted to alter the starts after the starts have been published. Competitors must notify to the Judges before the race is run that they have incurred a penalty, otherwise they will be disqualified and render themselves liable to suspension. Handicappers must state on their handicaps up to what date they are made, which must be published on the programme."

(*See Law* 12.)

For wins at distances up to and including 300 yards.

1 yd. for distances up to and including	.	.	.	120 yds.
2 yds.	"	over 120 yds. and up to and including		220 "
3 "	"	" 220 "	"	300 "

Winners at distances up to and including 300 yards not to carry penalties in handicaps over 300 yards.

For wins at distances over 300 yds. and up to and including 600 yds.

6 yds. for distances over 300 yds. and up to and including 600 yds.

Winners at distances over 300 yards and up to and including 600 yards, not to carry penalties in handicaps over 600 yards.

Scale of Penalties

For wins at distances over 600 yds. and up to and including 1000 yds.

} 8 yds. for distances over 600 yds. and up to and including 1000 yds.

Winners at distances over 600 yards and up to and including 1000 yards, not to carry penalties in handicaps over 1000 yards.

For wins at distances over 1000 yds. and up to and including 1 mile.

} 14 yds. for distances over 1000 yds. and up to and including 1 mile.

And for each succeeding mile or part of a mile.

} An additional 10 yards.

For Wins in Walking Races.

} 25 yards per mile.

Winners of 120 yards Handicaps over 10 flights of Hurdles to be penalised 2 yards in a similar competition.

The foregoing penalties to be increased by one-half after the second win.

Winners of hurdle handicaps at distances over 120 yards, and of Steeplechases, to be exempt from penalties.

Penalties shall not be enforced beyond the scratch mark, and do not apply to wins on the same day at the same meeting.

In all cases the actual scratch man shall be exempt from penalties.

In cases of dead-heats for first prizes, the dead-heaters shall each incur penalties for subsequent events according to scale, unless the dead-heat is run off.

In all cases where sports are postponed, winners of first prizes at subsequent sports held during the interval of postponement shall be penalised according to scale.

CHAPTER XX

Amateur Athletic Association's Laws and Recommendations

Laws for athletic meetings and competitions—Recommendations for clubs.

THE Laws of the A.A.A. for athletic meetings and competitions should be known to every amateur athlete, as ignorance of them may very easily lose him his amateur status, so I give them, reproduced by permission, from the Association's book of rules, with some valuable recommendations.

Laws for Athletic Meetings and Competitions.

(Rule XXIV. enacts, "That if any Club advertise their Sports 'under A.A.A. Laws' and then violate the said Laws, such Club shall be dealt with as the General Committee of the A.A.A. shall think fit.")

As to the Qualification of Competitors.

1. All competitions must be limited to Amateurs. This Law does not interfere with the right of any Club to refuse an entry to its own Sports.

"An Amateur is one who has never competed for a money prize, or monetary consideration, or for any declared wager or staked bet; who has never engaged in, assisted in, or taught any Athletic exercise as a means of pecuniary gain ; and who has never taken part in any competition with any one who is not an Amateur."

The following exceptions shall be made to this Law, viz. :—

(*a*) That Amateur athletes shall not lose their amateur status by competing with or against professionals in Cricket matches or in ordinary Club Football matches for which no prizes are given, or in Cup Competitions permitted by the National Football Associations or National Rugby Unions of England, Ireland, Scotland, or Wales, providing that such competitions or matches form no part of, nor have connection with any Athletic Meeting.

(*b*) That Competitions-at-arms between Volunteers and Regulars shall not be considered as coming within the scope of the A.A.A. Laws.

(*c*) That Competitors in Officers' Races at Naval and Military Athletic Meetings (such races being for officers only, and for which money prizes are not given) shall be exempt from the laws of the A.A.A. disqualifying runners for competing at mixed meetings.

(*d*) That the "Championship of the Army" Races be exempt from the effect of this Rule.

(*e*) That a paid handicapper is not a professional.

(*f*) That a competitor in athletic competitions (other than A.A.A. Championships or *bonâ fide* International, Inter-Club, Inter-Team, Inter-College, or Inter-School contests), who asks for or receives travelling expenses ceases to be an amateur. No Club, Society, or Managing Body promoting an athletic competition shall, either directly or indirectly, pay or offer a

As to Prizes

monetary consideration to, or the travelling expenses of, any competitor in such competition. Clubs, Colleges, or Schools shall be answerable for any payments made by them, and if called upon to do so shall produce full details of the same and accounts to the A.A.A. (North, South, or Midlands) Committee.

As to Prizes.

2. No "value" prize (*i.e.* a cheque on a tradesman) must be offered.

3. No prize must be offered in a Handicap of greater value than £10, 10s.

4. Every prize of the value of £5 or upwards must be engraved (when practicable) with the name and date of the meeting.

5. All prizes shall be of the full advertised value, that is, without discount, and must be publicly presented on the grounds on the day of the Sports.

6. That a fee of 5s. be lodged with all objections to the value of prizes, to be retained if the objection be considered frivolous.

7. In no case must a prize and money be offered as alternatives.

N.B.—No person must be allowed to compete while under a sentence of suspension passed by the A.A.A., National Cyclists' Union, Amateur Swimming Association, Amateur Gymnastic Association, Scottish A.A.A., or Irish A.A.A. (Rule x.).

All Clubs holding open handicap races shall employ an official handicapper (Rule xxviii.).

No one shall be allowed to compete at any meeting held under the Laws of the A.A.A. as "unattached" for more than one season (Rule xxix.).

Advertisements

Betting.

8. All open betting must be suppressed.

Advertisements.

9. All Clubs must hold their Sports "under the Laws of the Amateur Athletic Association," and so advertise them on all Prospectuses, Entry Forms, Programmes, &c., and *must* have printed on their Entry Forms "the definition of an Amateur." (*See Law* 1.)

That all affiliated clubs shall place on the advertisements, programmes, prospectuses, &c., of their meetings a statement that the club is so affiliated; and that all unaffiliated clubs or managing bodies to which a permit has been granted, shall also so state that the permit has been granted, and shall exhibit their certificates of registration or permit on the day of the meeting in a conspicuous place in the competitors' dressing-room.

Entries.

10. Sports Committees may reserve to themselves the right to refuse any entry, without being bound to assign a reason; or to disqualify a competitor at any time if his conversation or conduct is unbecoming, or if it is shown that his entry was made under false pretences.

11. All entries shall be made to the Secretary of the Sports, and entries made to the Handicapper shall be void.

No person shall be handicapped unless his entry form appears to be filled up in accordance with the requirements of the A.A.A.

Entries

12. Entries shall not be tendered or accepted without the stipulated fees. Any competitor winning a first prize in an open handicap shall be penalised for all handicaps in which he may compete during the four days following such wins, Sunday not included. (The scale of penalties may be obtained from this Association and is printed at the end of the book.) The penalties not to apply to the scratch mark. No person, other than the handicapper, shall be permitted to alter the starts after the starts have been published. Competitors must notify to the Judges before the race is run that they have incurred a penalty, otherwise they will be disqualified and render themselves liable to suspension. Handicappers to state on their Handicaps up to what date they are made, which must be published on the programme. No one shall be permitted to start for a scratch race unless his name is printed on the programme, nor for a handicap event unless his name and handicap allowance are so recorded.

Competitors in Handicap Competitions shall be required to send with their entries full and definite particulars of (1) the last four events in which they have competed; (2) their last performance at each of the distances entered for; and (3) the last heat or prize won by them at each of the distances entered for. No club shall be affiliated to the Association or registered as "approved" unless it agrees to adopt the A.A.A. Entry Form.

No one shall be permitted to compete in any trial heat other than that in which his name is printed on the programme, and no made up, late, or supplementary heat or trials shall be permitted under any circumstances.

Protests

13. All entries shall be made in the real name of the competitor, and this name shall appear on the programme.

Youths and Novices.

14. Competitors in Youths' races must state their age and previous performances, and, if required, must furnish certificates of birth. Races for Youths, other than club races, shall be confined to boys under 15, resident for three months prior to the sports within a radius of three miles from the ground of the promoting club, and entries from boys under this age shall not be accepted for open events. This rule not to apply to boys attending schools and competing within 20 miles of Charing Cross, London. The age of boys (months and years) must appear on the programme of the day. For Novices' races, a novice is held to be one who, at the time of competing, has never won a prize in a similar class of competition—*i.e.* winning a prize for walking would not disqualify for running, or *vice versâ;* but winning a prize for running any distance would disqualify for running. (N.B.—The clause as to Novices does not apply to School and Boys' races.)

Protests.

15. All Protests against a competitor or against a competitor's qualification to compete, shall be made to the Secretary of the Club, in writing, before the prizes are distributed; and if the protest shall not be made good within one calendar month the prizes shall be awarded. Every protest must be accompanied with a deposit of five shillings, which shall be forfeited in case the same shall appear upon investigation to have been made on no reasonable ground.

Starting

Stations.

16. In Handicaps, stations shall be awarded according to the number on the programme.

Attendants.

17. No attendant shall accompany any competitor on the scratch (except in cycle races), nor in the race; nor shall a competitor be allowed, without the permission of the Judges, to receive assistance or refreshment from any one during the progress of a race. In cycle races attendants will be allowed for the sole purpose of lending assistance in starting. Any attendant who steps or follows the machine over the mark of the competitor whom he is assisting to start will cause such competitor to be disqualified.

Fouling.

18. Wilfully jostling or running across or obstructing another, so as to impede his progress, shall disqualify the offender.

Starting.

19. All questions as to starts shall be in the absolute discretion of the starter. All races (except time handicaps) shall be started by the report of a pistol. A start shall only be made to the actual report of the pistol. The starter shall place the competitors on their allotted marks, and shall, if necessary, have the assistance of marksmen for this duty. No competitor shall touch the ground in front of his mark with any part of his body. If any one competitor overstep his mark before the pistol has been fired the starter shall put him back one yard for distances up to and in-

High Jump and Pole Jump

cluding 220 yards, two yards up to and including 440 yards, three yards up to and including 880 yards, and five yards up to one mile or more. These penalties to be doubled for a second offence, and disqualification to follow a repetition of the same offence. (Committees of Sports are specially desired to print this rule *in extenso* on their Sports Programme.)

Walking Races.

20. In walking races, cautions and disqualifications shall be left to the decision of the judges of walking, who may appoint assistants if necessary. A disqualified competitor shall at once leave the track.

The High Jump and Pole Jump.

21. Each competitor shall be allowed three jumps at each height. Crossing the scratch without displacing the bar shall not count as one jump. All measurements shall be made from the ground to the centre of the bar. In the High Jump neither diving nor somersaulting shall be permitted. The cross-bars shall be of wood only, of a uniform thickness throughout, and without weights. The maximum projection of the pegs shall be 3 inches from the uprights. The ends of the cross-bar shall not project more than six inches from the pegs. In the pole jump three attempts, even if the cross-bar be not displaced, shall count as one jump.

The Broad Jump.

Each competitor shall be allowed three jumps, and the best three competitors of the first trial shall be allowed three more tries each for the final. The farthest jump of the six attempts shall win. If any competitor fall back or step back, after jumping, or crosses the taking-off line with either foot, or so swerves aside that he pass beyond the taking-off line, such jump shall not be measured, but it shall be counted against the competitor as one jump. All jumps shall be measured to the taking-off line from the edge of the heel-mark nearest that line, along a line perpendicular to that line. The taking-off line shall be of wood.

Steeplechasing.

22. For Steeplechases the hurdles shall not be higher than 3 feet. Every competitor must go over or through the water: and any one who jumps to one side or the other of the water jump shall be disqualified.

Throwing the Cricket Ball.

23. In throwing the Cricket Ball, the distance thrown shall be calculated from the centre of a scratch line; and the thrower, in delivering the ball, shall not cross such scratch line. Three tries only shall be allowed, and crossing the scratch shall count as one try.

Winners of Trial heats.

24. That winners of trial heats must compete in the finals, unless the consent of the Judges to their abstention has been obtained, or become liable to suspension.

25. That the Secretary of every race meeting shall send a marked copy of the programme of the meeting

First-Claim Law

to the Secretary of the A.A.A. division within which the meeting is held; and in the event of a mixed meeting, also to the Secretary of the local centre of the N.C.U. These programmes are to be filed and to be open for inspection by all athletes at reasonable hours.

26. That no entry shall be made or accepted unless a form of entry authorised by the A.A.A. be used.

27. That all club handicaps shall be made from the actual scratch man in the race.

First-claim Law.

28. In any Inter-Club contest advertised "for first-claim men under A.A.A. Laws," where no other definition of first-claim men has been previously given, each competitor must have been a member of the club he represents at least three months immediately prior to the race; and in the event of his residing more than twenty miles from the head-quarters of his club, he must have been a member for one year immediately prior to the race. When a man is a member of two or more competing clubs, the club which can show the longest unbroken period of his present membership has first claim upon his services.

N.B.—" That the N.C.A.A.A and M.C.A.A.A. and the Southern Committee have power to make and enforce bye-laws and regulations in their respective districts, subject to the veto of the General Committee of the A.A.A." (Rule xxxiv.).

Recommendations for Clubs

In addition to the foregoing, the following RULES FOR COMPETITIONS and the MANAGEMENT OF ATHLETIC SPORTS, adopted by the Amateur Athletic Association, are RECOMMENDED to Clubs holding Sports under the Laws of the A.A.A. :—

Officials.

29. The officials of a meeting shall consist of: A Committee, in whose hands shall be placed all matters which do not relate to the actual conduct of the meeting itself, and who shall have a final decision in all cases not provided for in the rules of the meeting.

Two or more Judges, whose joint decision shall be final in every competition, and with whom shall rest the power to disqualify any competitior.

A Referee, who shall decide in the event of a difference of opinion between the Judges. The decision of the Referee shall be final in all cases.

Two or more Stewards, or Clerks of the Course, whose business shall be to call out the competitors for each event, and to assign to each his distinctive Badge.

One or more special Judges of Walking, a Timekeeper, a Starter, and one or more Marksmen.

Stations.

30. Competitors in level races shall draw lots for their respective places on the post before leaving the dressing-room. Each competitor shall be supplied with and wear during each contest a distinctive number corresponding to his number in the programme.

31. Only the winners of the trial heats (first round)

in sprint handicaps run over a stringed track shall be eligible for further competition. In cases where the track is not stringed and in distance races the first and second, or first, second, and third, may compete in second round or final heats, at the option of the Judges.

Track Measurements.

32. All tracks shall be measured twelve inches from the inner side of the path.

Clothing.

33. Every competitior must wear complete clothing from the shoulders to the knees (*e.g.* sleeved jersey and loose drawers).

Any competitor may be excluded from taking part in the sports unless properly attired.

Straight Sprint Races.

34. Straight Sprint Races shall be run on a part of the cinder path or grass so staked and stringed that each competitor may have a separate course. The width between the strings shall not be less than four feet, and the stakes shall not be less than thirty feet apart.

Hurdle Races.

35. The Hurdle Race shall be over ten flights of hurdles on a level grass course of 120 yards straight. The hurdles shall stand 3ft. 6in. from the ground, and shall have level toprails, and shall be placed 10 yards apart. The first flight of hurdles shall be 15 yards from scratch. Each competitor shall have his own line of hurdles, and shall keep to that line throughout the race.

Putting the Weight

Throwing the Hammer.

36. The Hammer shall be thrown from within a circle of 9 ft. in diameter. The head of the hammer shall be of iron or lead, or both, and spherical, and the handle shall be of wood or metal, or both. The head and handle shall weigh together 16 lbs. The total length of the hammer shall be not more than 4 ft., and no cross-piece, ring or loop at the end of the handle shall be allowed. Each competitor shall be allowed three throws, and the best three competitors of the first trial shall be allowed three more throws each. The farthest throw of the six shall win. All distances shall be measured from the circumference of the circle to the first pitch of the hammer along a line drawn from that pitch to the centre of the circle.

Putting the Weight.

37. The Weight shall be put from the shoulder with one hand only, and without follow from a 7 ft. square. The weight shall be of iron and spherical, and shall weigh 16 lbs. All puts shall be measured perpendicularly from the first pitch of the weight to the front line of the square, or to that line produced. Each competitor shall be allowed three puts, and the best three competitors of the first trial shall be allowed three more puts each. The farthest put of the six shall win.

38. In Throwing the Hammer and Putting the Weight crossing the scratch shall count as a try.

Tug-of-War.

39. The teams shall consist of equal numbers of competitors. The rope shall be of sufficient length to allow for a "pull" of twelve feet, and for twelve feet slack at each end, together with four feet for each

competitor; it shall not be less than four inches in circumference, and shall be without knots or other holdings for the hands. A centre tape shall be affixed to the centre of the rope, and six feet on each side of the centre tape two side tapes shall be affixed to the rope. A centre line shall be marked on the ground, and six feet on either side of the centre line two side lines parallel thereto. At the start the rope shall be taut, and the centre tape shall be over the centre line, and the competitors shall be outside the side lines.

The start shall be by word of mouth. During no part of the pull shall the foot of any competitor go beyond the centre line. The pull shall be won when one team shall have pulled the side tape of the opposing side over their own side line. No competitor shall wear boots or shoes with any projecting nails, springs, or points of any kind. No competitor shall make any hole in the ground with his feet, or in any other way before the start. No competitor shall wilfully touch the ground with any part of his person but his feet. If the competition is for teams limited in weight, each competitor shall be weighed before the start. The final heat shall be won by two pulls out of three.

Level 300 and 440 Yards Hurdle Races on Grass.

40. (1) No Record can be made on any track that does not comply with the following conditions: (2) There shall be 10 flights of hurdles in each distance. (3) Each competitor shall keep his own flight of hurdles throughout. Hurdles to be 3 ft. out of ground, with straight top-bars. (4) No competitor shall be allowed a record unless he break the worsted, so that a correct time can be taken. (5) Each track of hurdles must be measured the correct and full distance to the winning

post. In 300 yard races—(6) The first hurdle shall be 45 yards from each competitor's scratch mark, and the remaining hurdles shall be as near as possible 25 yards apart. The distance from the last hurdle to the winning post shall be 30 yards. In 440 yard races—(7) The first hurdle shall be placed 50 yards from each competitor's scratch mark, and the remaining hurdles shall be as nearly as possible 40 yards apart, and the distance from the last hurdle to the winning post shall be 30 yards. (8) The last 75 yards, if possible, should be straight. (*See Record Rules, page* 36.)

Programmes, &c.

41. The A.A.A. recommend that a programme of any proposed meeting (showing the entrants for, and the starts allotted in each event) shall be forwarded by post to each entrant, to the address given in his entry form, and shall be posted not later than the day before the day appointed for the meeting, or that such programme as aforesaid shall be advertised the day next before the day appointed for the meeting in one of the public papers circulating in the district of the proposed meeting.

42. It is recommended that all Athletic Clubs and Sports Committees have the following notice conspicuously printed on their entry forms and programmes :—

"The prizes offered at this meeting will be awarded subject to the statements of previous performances given on the entry forms being strictly accurate."

Index

Index

Printed by BALLANTYNE, HANSON & Co.
Edinburgh & London

Useful Guides to
Entertaining in Public & Private.

Modern Card Manipulation

By C. LANG NEIL.

With upwards of 100 Illustrations.

Price 1s., *post free* **1s. 2d.**

Contains Explanations of all the best Card Tricks of the leading Conjurers. The tricks are illustrated with actual Photographs taken at the various stages of performance, and thus the amateur is enabled to follow the methods employed with the greatest ease.

After-Dinner Sleights and Pocket Tricks

By C. LANG NEIL.

Price 1s., *post free* **1s. 2d.**

With upwards of 100 Illustrations.

A Collection of Amusing Tricks, requiring very little skill, and no, or very simple, apparatus. These Tricks are, as the title suggests, especially suitable for a few minutes' amusement after dinner, or to fill up what might become an awkward pause, as the time occupied in the presentation of each is very short.

Boy's and Girl's Reciter

Cloth, **Price 1s.,** *post free* **1s. 2d.**

A collection of the very best Recitations, Stories, etc., by well-known authors, including Selections from Rudyard Kipling, Tennyson, A. A. Proctor, Jean Ingelow, J. T. Fields, W. W. Jacobs, J. K. Jerome, Barry Pain, Clement Scott, etc.

The Drawing-Room Entertainer

A Practical Guide to the Art of Amateur and Semi-Professional Entertaining.

By CECIL H. BULLIVANT.

Cloth,

Price 1s.,

post free

1s. 2d.

The Contents include:— Ventriloquism — Conjuring — Popular Entertainments — The Drawing Room Comedian — The Sketch Artist — Variety Programmes — Methods and Management — How Best to Secure Engagements.

Speeches for all Occasions

By AN OXFORD M.A.

Cloth, **Price 1s.,** *post free* **1s. 2d.**

Including suitable Toasts for Festive Gatherings, Duties of a Chairman, Rules and Subjects for Debating Clubs, etc.

Pearson's Temperance Reciter

Readings and Recitations for Bands of Hope, Temperance Societies, and P.S.A. Meetings.

Containing choice selections from the writings of:—Sir A. Conan Doyle, Geo. R. Sims, Silas Hocking, Jerome K. Jerome, Clement Scott, J. G. Whittier, and many others.

Cloth, **Price 1s.,** *post free* **1s. 2d.**

The above volumes may be had of all Booksellers, or post free from the Publishers,
C. Arthur Pearson, Ltd., 17–18 Henrietta Street, London, W.C.

CHARACTER READING AND FORTUNE TELLING.

Pearson's Dream Book

BY PROFESSOR P. R. S. FOLI,

Cloth, **Price 1s.,** *post free* **1s. 2d.**

Some of the subjects dealt with are:—
Dreams and their Mystic Reality—The Interpretation of Dreams by Magic Ciphers—The Magic Square of Fate—A Table of Dreams according to their Days—A List of Dreams, Subjects, and what they indicate, alphabetically arranged—Omens, etc.

Fortune Teller

BY PROFESSOR P. R. S. FOLI.

Cloth, **Price 1s.,** *post free* **1s. 2d.**

The subjects dealt with include:—
Augury by Birds—Astrology—Gipsy Fortune-tellers — Crystal Gazing — Advice and Hints for Beginners in Fortune-telling — Lucky Stars — Lines on the Hand in Palmistry— Precious Stones and their Meanings—Rings and Bridecake—Wedding Rings—Teacup Fortune-telling—Good and Bad Luck—Quaint Ceremonies, etc.

Fortune Telling by Cards

BY PROFESSOR P. R. S. FOLI.

Cloth,

Price 1s.,

post free

1s. 2d.

This Volume includes all the best known methods of Reading the Cards.

Hands And How to Read Them

BY E. RENÉ.

Cloth, **Price 1s.,** *post free* **1s. 2d.**

Some of the Contents of this book are:—

Fingers as the Indicators of Talents, etc. — Evidence of Will-power in the Thumb — The Mounts and their Characteristics — Hands Devoid of Lines & Covered with Lines — Principal Lines & their Meanings— Rules for Reading the Hands— Signs of Good and Bad Health —Cause of Unhappy Marriages —How Palmistry Can Help—Predictions in Regard to Love and Marriage—The Line of Fame or Fortune, etc., etc.

Handwriting as an Index to Character

BY PROFESSOR P. R. S. FOLI.

With numerous Illustrations.

Cloth, **Price 1s.,** *post free* **1s. 2d.**

By comparing your writing with specimens given in the book you will be able at a glance to read your own character.

Examples are given of famous people in all walks of life, and their handwriting is critically examined for indications of temperament, etc.

Heads And How to Read Them

A Popular Guide to Phrenology.

BY STACKPOOL E. O'DELL,

The Eminent Phrenologist.

With 80 Illustrations.

Cloth, **Price 1s.,** *post free* **1s. 2d.**

Some of the Contents of this Useful Hand-book are:—
The Aspiring Head — The Domestic Head—How to Discern Temperaments—How to be Happy—Intellectual Heads—Mechanical and Business Heads — Men Women Ought and Ought Not to Marry—The Professional Head—The Reflective Head—A Born Cook—A Servant who will do Her Best—How to Choose Servants—Head showing Activity, Matrimonial Temperament, Refined Mind, Vitality, etc.

The above volumes may be had of all Booksellers, or post free from the Publishers,
C. Arthur Pearson, Ltd., 17-18 Henrietta Street, London, W.C.

The GARDEN & HOME PETS

Small Gardens

And How to make the Most of Them.

By VIOLET P. BIDDLE. *Cloth,* **Price 1s.,** *post free* **1s. 2d.**

A most useful Handbook for the Amateur. Full instructions are given for laying-out, bedding, arrangement of borders, vegetable culture, flowers and fruit, and trees, room plants, window boxes, etc.

Roses

And How to Grow Them.

By VIOLET P. BIDDLE. *Cloth,* **Price 1s.,** *post free* **1s. 2d.**

The Contents include:—Preparing Beds and Borders—Select Garden Roses—Planting Out—Climate and the Rose—Pruning—Budding—Climbing Roses—Pillar Roses—Rose Hedges—Roses for Shady Places—Roses for Towns—Rose Pergolas—Late Roses—Carpets for Roses—Rose Enemies—Roses as Cut Flowers—Roses by Post—Roses for Exhibition, etc., etc.

Greenhouses

How to Make and Manage Them.

By WILLIAM F. ROWLES. With numerous Diagrams.

Cloth, **Price 1s.,** *post free* **1s. 2d.**

Some of the 22 Chapters deal with:—House Construction—The Heating Question—Working up Stock—Propagation—Pots and Potting—Soils and Manures—Watering—Shading—Tying and Staking—Syringing—Training—Pinching and Pruning—Arranging—Forcing—Critical Periods in Plant Life—Specialisation, etc., etc.

Rabbit Keeping

For Pleasure and Profit.

By GEORGE GARDNER, With 12 Illustrations. *Cloth,* **Price 1s.,** *post free* **1s. 2d.**

Poultry Keeping

And How to Make it Pay.

By F. E. WILSON. *Cloth,* **Price 1s.,** *post free* **1s. 2d.**

The information given includes:—Natural and Artificial Hatching—The Rearing and Management of Chickens—Housing, Feeding and Exhibiting Poultry—Breeding for Egg Production—Ducks for Profit, etc.

THE . . DOG

In Health and Disease By F. M. ARCHER. With 12 Illustrations By S. T. DADD, *Cloth,* **Price 1s.,** *post free* **1s. 2d.**

THE DOG IN HEALTH & DISEASE

BY F. M. ARCHER

Cage and Singing Birds

By GEORGE GARDNER. With numerous Illustrations. *Cloth,* **Price 1s.,** *post free* **1s. 2d.**

CAGE AND SINGING BIRDS

GEORGE GARDNER

Some of the Contents are:—Birds for song, for exhibition, and for Breeding—care of young—Seeds, how and what to buy—Moulting for song and for exhibition—Colour-feeding; how it is done—Diseases of Cage Birds and how to treat them—Bird fever—Parasites and how to destroy them, etc., etc.

The above volumes may be had of all Booksellers, or post free from the Publishers, C. Arthur Pearson, Ltd., 17–18 Henrietta Street, London, W.C.